Michael J. Durkin

DOUBLE
Your
Contacts

What Every Network Marketer
Needs To Know About
Making Contacts And Booking Appointments.

II

Michael J. Durkin
Sales Judo Academy
Office: 1-866-350-6477
Email: mdurkin@salesjudo.com
Website: www.salesjudo.com
Book website: www.doubleyourcontacts.com

Copyright 2005 Michael J. Durkin

ISBN: 0-9736187-9-5

For Corey Michael and Tyler Michael

Introduction

This book is the result of almost 20 years of research. It contains cutting edge technology that runs counter to most of the conventional sales wisdom promulgated over the last 50 years.

And that it is why it works!

However, most people will not use this material the way it is intended. They will read this book thinking that they will magically acquire the beliefs and skills needed to be successful at contacting.

If you use the book this way, you are fooling yourself. You should call me and get your money back. I'm not kidding! Here are 5 things you need to examine before you read this book. If you can't commit to these 5 things, I want you to put the book down and call me toll-free at 1-866-350-6477 and ask my office for a refund. I'll tell you what to say after you read these five points:

1. You must be at the point in your business where you truly believe that your ability to put people on a list, call them and book an appointment is the most critical thing you must do to succeed. If you believe that learning how to show the opportunity, using the products, getting on standing orders, etc. are the keys to success in your Network Marketing Business, then you are not ready for the maximum benefit this book has to offer and you should call me to get your money back.

2. Some of you bought this book because you read the bullet points advertising the "secrets" to

contacting and you said to yourself, "Wow! I want to see if that really is a 'secret' on page 17. What you will do is read the book quickly to see if you agree or disagree with the "secrets." You will then say to yourself, "Oh I already know that one" or " I already do that. I thought I was going to learn something new!" The problem is that you will actually believe yourself. You will make a judgment in your own mind whether or not what you just read will be effective. If you bought the book to see if YOU were right, then you are not ready. Please get a refund and use your money to buy one of your own products or a motivational CD from your upline.

3. You must be willing to risk! My material flies in the face of all conventional theories on booking appointments. It is going to seem somewhat edgy, daring and even crazy at first. You are going to have to trust me for a bit. Some of you won't actually try the techniques until you get backed into a corner with a prospect or you decide you have nothing to lose. That's okay! You're going to have to be willing to try something new and see how it works. It really is going to come down to this for some of you: "How sick am I to not have my calendar full?" Your willingness to take risks will be in direct correlation to how disgusted you are with yourself! If you are looking at your calendar and you don't have at least an average of one appointment per day booked for the next two weeks you should be skeeved out! If you're not, you probably are not going to be willing to take risks and you should get your money back.

4. In order to "master" these techniques you are

going to have to read Double Your Contacts at least 5 times! You're going to have to use this book as a reference and come back to it again and again. Many of the strategies and techniques will look deceptively simple and trite when they are in print. You'll have a tendency to bypass a powerful phrase or idea because it's only 5 words or it just isn't complicated enough for you! Imbedded in this material is a secret that some of you are ready to hear. You will take it and run with it. Most people don't find it until they have read the book a minimum of 5 times! Don't miss this one!

5. You must be willing to fail! I know most of you will hate this, but it is an essential part of the process to becoming a prospecting machine and living the life your Network Marketing business can provide for you. You have to try this material and strategies when cold-contacting or making phone calls and be completely willing to screw it up! You need to get to the point where you enjoy screwing it up. As you are applying the techniques in this book you will experience a phenomenon I call "contacting interruptus." You will start using methods from the book and you'll get some interest or at least you'll get farther along with a prospect than you ever have before...........and then you'll get stuck. You won't know which way to turn next. Or your prospect will hit you with something you didn't expect and you'll go down in flames. You'll be upset, but your support team and I will be ecstatic! You need to bring this scenario back to your support team and ask them what the next step should have been. Then you take that lesson, incorporate it into your prospecting and try again!

Double Your Contacts: What Every NM Needs To Know About Making Contacts And Booking Appointments
©Michael J. Durkin

And again, and again!

There is no magic book that will fill your calendar automatically just by reading it. Are you clear? Good. Now if you cannot agree with these 5 steps and commit to doing them, then reading the book even once is a waste of time. Would you agree with that? Call my office and say, "Hi this is _____. MJ oversold me with his promotion and I believed that I would become a great prospector by just reading the book once. I didn't think I would have to work at it. I thought it would be easy, and that a book would automatically solve all my prospecting problems. I promise to use the book I just bought to start my next fire if you would be nice enough to remove the charge from my credit card."

I'm not kidding. You should and we will.

If you're still with me, let's get to work.

MJ Durkin

P.S. I have just started to introduce you to one of the major secrets to successful prospecting if you were ready to see it, hear it and feel it.

P.P.S. Don't worry if you didn't get it yet! Keep reading!

TABLE OF CONTENTS

Belief Systems About Contacting: Are They Helping You or Hurting You?

In this section I'm going to teach you the belief systems that you will need to be successful at contacting and booking meetings

Chapter 1: Belief Systems versus Techniques - Which is more Important?

If I have a hundred salespeople in a room and ask them, "What do you want to learn today?" what do you think they would answer? Do you think they would ask to learn something about the way they think about selling? That they would want to get their beliefs or attitudes straightened out? You're right if you said, "No". Typically out of one hundred different professions, I hear they want to learn some kind of technique that will help them close a sale. They almost never say, "Well, I have some beliefs about making phone calls that are really hurting my ability to prospect, and I need to deal with that." My trainees always want a technique-based solution because they think there are some magic words, some silver bullet that will get the prospect to say, "Yes."

Every salesperson I train wants the technique because they believe people make decisions based on what is said to the prospect. They think that it is the "words" that per-suade and convince people. Most sales gurus have fallen into this trap. They tend to give their audiences what they ask for. So they write books and give seminars with all kinds of fancy techniques to "close" the deal. Neil Rackham, the author of **Spin Selling**, said a business publisher once told him that if a book title didn't have the word "close" in it, he wouldn't consider publishing it because no salesperson would buy it! Teaching closing techniques and one-liners is flashy, glitzy and fun. They keep an audience entertained but are rarely used by the trainees outside of the seminar because it takes specific belief systems to actually execute these "magical" phrases!

You have belief systems about everything in your life,

even at the simplest level. For example: Most people have a belief system that if they are in a room where a light is off and they go to a light switch and flip it up, that a light will come on. No rocket science here, but why do most people have that belief? Experience has proven to them time and time again this is the most probable result when they take that action. You believe when you go to apply the brake on your car that it will stop. You believe that your mother will call about 2 months before Christmas and start lobbying you about your plans for the holidays. Why? Years of experience tell us that these things are true. (My own mother usually calls right after Halloween to start the big push).

Belief Systems: For you or against you?

Let me assure you...you have ALL kinds of beliefs surrounding your involvement in your Network Marketing business. You have beliefs about the reactions you are going to get from your friends and relatives. You have beliefs about your upline, about the products and about the company. You have beliefs about contacting, calling people on the phone, showing the opportunity, speaking in public and signing people up. You have belief systems around your confidence, your abilities, your strengths and your weaknesses. You have a belief about every aspect of yourself and this business. I'm about to give you some good news and some bad news.

You have belief systems that either support your ability to do your business or you have belief systems that are non-supportive of your ability to be successful in your Network Marketing business. Let's look at some negative belief systems you'll hear me refer to as "head trash" that people can have about this business. Since this book is about contacting and booking meetings, I'll focus there. See if you hear any of these voices in your head:

"I don't like to call people on the phone."

"I don't like calling people and bothering them at night."

"It's rude to call someone at home at night- I might interrupt their dinner."

"I hate it when people call me at night and talk business or try to sell me something."

"I hate telemarketers – Why do they always call during dinner?"

"I don't even answer my phone at home – I always look at the caller ID first."

"What if I call and they are busy – They won't be able to listen to me anyway."

"I don't meet any new people during the day."

"I don't like it when people I don't know try to strike up conversations with me and I don't feel comfortable trying to talk to someone I don't know."

"Salespeople are pushy. I don't want to be known as a "salesperson"

"I hate cold contacting."

"I don't know anybody who would be interested in this business"

"I can't think of anyone to put on a list."

"I don't like to ask people to buy things."

"Selling things to your friends and neighbors is rude."

"My friends will laugh at me or think I'm crazy to have gotten into a business like this."

"I'm uncomfortable "pitching" my friends about this."

"I'm not a salesperson."

"I don't want to bother people."

"A networking marketing person hounded me years ago. I don't want to be like them."

"I hate rejection."

"I like everything about the business except the prospecting."

Do any of these ring a bell for you? Don't be nervous. It's not unusual for professional salespeople who make their living selling to have these kinds of belief systems. So don't be too concerned if you do. This is very normal even if you've been in the business for a while. But you can see that these belief systems are extremely non-supportive of your ability to contact and book appointments. Most of you want me to teach you a magical technique that will obviate these negative beliefs and render them powerless. The problem here is that some of these beliefs are so ingrained in you that even if I teach you powerful techniques that WILL work, you won't have the strength or fortitude to execute them.

Don't get me wrong here. It's possible to use techniques to make your beliefs stronger and more supportive. By consistently applying technique and having some successes, your belief system will start to automatically rewrite itself. When you try one of my techniques and you actually have a success, your belief in your ability goes up a notch and you're willing to try it again with stronger conviction. Dale Carnegie used this method in the early days of his public speaking course. He knew that most of his students were terrified of speaking in front of any audience consisting of two or more people. So his first step was to have each student give a 2-minute introduction of who they were to their own classmates in the course. Some of them almost passed out! They then progressed to a 5-minute talk, 10-minute talk and so on. Then he slowly increased the audience size until at the end of a year (52 speeches) his students' belief in themselves enabled them to give 1-hour talks to audiences of over 100 people!

So rewriting your belief systems CAN be done by consistent application and repetition of systematic technique. My problem with this method is that it is incredibly inefficient and agonizingly slow! I can't stand doing things slowly! I don't have time to wait - and neither do you. So let's start fixing your head trash right away with my method for developing belief systems that support your ability to prospect.

The first and most important step is identifying the beliefs and challenges you have with prospecting. Once you have clearly identified them you can consciously start to rewrite them. The problem is most of your non-supportive belief systems are sabotaging you on an unconscious level. So let's get them out in the open so we can start to take away their power. Turn to the next page and take the Prospecting Beliefs Self- Assessment.

Prospecting Beliefs Self–Assessment

First check off the beliefs that apply to you. As you read each statement you will actually recognize the voice in your head saying these things. Then in the dollar sign space next to each statement, try to estimate how much that non-supportive belief system is "costing" you over the course of a year. One way to figure out the amount is to say to yourself, "If I was to get this issue handled so that it didn't stop me from doing what I need to do to be able to reach_____ level in the business, that would be worth_____ amount of income per year. That figure is the one you put in the dollar sign space. This figure is what it's "costing" you per year NOT to get it done.

❑ I like everything about the business except the prospecting part. $_____

❑ When I call someone, I don't know if they will be interested and I hate the idea they might be aggravated or upset with me for calling them. $_____

❑ I don't have time to prospect and do it right. $_____

❑ I don't like to be bothered at night on the phone and I don't like to bother others. $_____

❑ I don't like having to call my friends. $_____

❑ I feel like I'm interrupting people when I call. $_____

❑ I don't want to look foolish or stupid if they say no. $_____

❑ I need people to like me and approve of me. $_____

❑ I'm afraid that if they give me an objection I can't handle I'll look dumb. $_____

❑ Everyone has already been approached by some $_____
multi-level business. They don't need me talking to
them about another one.

❑ I can't think of anyone who would be interested $_____

❑ It's rude to call people at night and interrupt their $_____
relaxation time.

❑ I don't like it when MY phone rings at night and $_____
people want to talk business.

❑ I'm not good on the phone. I get nervous and $_____
don't know what to say.

❑ I don't want to hound people like some pesky $_____
Network Marketing person.

❑ I can't stand "network-marketing types" $_____
they're always so darn happy!

❑ I just plain hate calling people to set up $_____
appointments.

❑ Showing the business is fine. It's putting the $_____
people on the list I don't like.

❑ What my friends think of me and the way I make $_____
my living is important to me.

❑ I don't like "selling" to my friends, relatives $_____
and neighbors.

Go back over the prospecting beliefs and circle the
three that are the most prevalent and really damaging
to your ability to prospect. In the ($_____) space at
the end of the statements you circled, write in the dollar
amount this problem is costing you in commission
income over the course of a year.

Double Your Contacts: What Every NM Needs To Know About Making Contacts And Booking Appointments
©Michael J. Durkin

Add up the three numbers you placed in the ($_____)
spaces and place the total here ⌐

These beliefs are costing me | $ | in residual income
per year.

**When you look at this number how does it make
you feel? Did you realize these beliefs were costing
you that much? Does it make you mad to think how
much these beliefs are preventing you from making?
If you had this money, would many of your dreams be
coming true?**

While this exercise has the potential to leave you
depressed, my hope is that you are mad – hopping mad!
Mad at yourself for letting these beliefs control you and
keep you from your dreams. Can you see how these
belief systems hold you back and are non-supportive of
your ability to book appointments? Can you see how they
are the mother of all your prospecting issues? Can you
see how they keep you from making a list and getting on
the phone? Is it clear to you now why you just keep putting off your prospecting?

These belief systems are recorded just as firmly in your
brain and in your heart as any recording on a compact
disc. They will replay in your subconscious over and over
again. How often have you been doing something benign
like mowing the lawn or taking a shower and a song
popped into your head? Not one that you heard that
morning on the radio but one that you haven't heard in ten
years or even since you were a child. You find yourself
humming or singing along and think, "Where did that come
from? I haven't even heard that song in 20 years!" That's

the power of the subconscious mind. As you remember the song you might even have a certain feeling or smell a familiar odor. The recording etched on the tracks of your mind never really goes away, does it? It can come back without any notice and bring positive energy or negative baggage with it. This is powerful stuff that controls our behavior and it's very insidious because we don't even know it's happening.

Just taking the time to recognize and admit you have these beliefs reduces their power over you by 50%. If you can really see and feel how much they are costing you, they should tumble by another 25%. Now, let's wipe out the other 25%!

Re-writing Non-Supportive Belief Systems

Picture your mind as a compact disc recording with these non-supportive beliefs on it. Imagine you were to take a screwdriver or nail file and just scratch it wildly over the surface of the disk. In effect you would be rendering the disc unreadable and it would not play, correct? Now you need to re-record over it and etch the **NEW** beliefs into the tracks. Find your three most damaging beliefs about prospecting. Write them down on numbers 1, 2 and 3 below. (Leave 1b, 2b and 3b blank for now).

1. _____

1b. _____

2. _____

2b. _____

3. _____

3b. _____

Now cross out the non-supportive belief system with your pen and rewrite a supportive belief system under b. of each number. For example:

1. I'm not good on the phone. I get nervous and I don't know what to say.

1b. I love the phone. I'm awesome on the phone. I never get nervous and I always know what to say!

Or

2. It's rude to call people at home and interrupt their relaxation time.

2b. People do business at night on the phone ALL the time. I do it and I'm used to it. Everyone understands that some business needs to get done by phone at home. I like calling people at home and introducing them to something that can change their life!

If you had to guess when the right time to do this exercise is, when do you think it would be? Yes, right now! Once you have come up with 3 new supportive beliefs take out a business card and write them on the back of one. Put it back in your wallet or purse. Pull it out twice a day and read these statements out loud to yourself. Once in the morning and once in the evening. Write them on an index card and post them on your dashboard or on your mirror and practice saying them out loud twice a day for thirty days. I guarantee you'll crush them and render them powerless.

Chapter 2: Techniques Reinforce Belief – How Strong Are Yours?

If your belief systems are strong and powerful you literally do not need good Technique. Any high level successful distributor in your network hierarchy will tell you that out of their conviction and belief came some of their best material. They got challenged, and because their belief was rock-solid they handled objections automatically and then said, "Wow, that was pretty good stuff!" Technique does play a part in reinforcing beliefs that support your ability to contact, make calls and book appointments. Let's look at the strength of your techniques.

Prospecting Techniques: Self-Assessment

First check off the technique issues that apply to you. Then in the dollar sign next to each statement try to estimate how much that non-supportive belief is "costing" you over the course of a year. One way to figure out the amount is to say to yourself, "If I had this issue handled so it didn't stop me from doing what I need to do to be able to reach_____level in the business, that would be worth $_____amount of income per year. This figure is what it is "costing" you per year NOT to get it done.

❑ Not getting enough referrals from people $_____
who don't get in.

❑ Inconsistent prospecting behavior. $_____

❑ Get cornered answering questions and $_____
talking too much when making a cold contact.

❑ Don't have a system for tracking daily, $_____
when I'm making calls and when I'm not.

❑ Don't have enough prospects on my list. $_____

❑ Don't have a written list of prospects. $_____

❑ Difficulty dealing with the "Call me in a month $_____
   or so when I'm not so busy" stall.

❑ Do not have a handwritten prospect list $_____
   on my person at all times.

❑ Can't get prospects live on the phone. $_____

❑ Can't get them to return voice mail messages. $_____

❑ Freeze up when I get a cold response, $_____
   negativity or no response as I start to launch
   into the reason I called.

❑ Can't find a quiet, business-like atmosphere to $_____
   make my calls from.

❑ Can go a whole week without making a phone $_____
   call or making a cold contact.

❑ Getting prompted to give your presentation over $_____
   the phone.

❑ Fear of picking up the phone. $_____

❑ Just plain "hate" cold contacting and phone $_____
   calling.

❑ Hear that I have obviously interrupted someone $_____
   by calling and don't' know how to handle it.

❑ Get caught sending prospects to web sites or $_____
   sending literature instead of getting
   appointments.

❑ Can't handle the "I'm too busy or I'm $_____
   doing okay in my job" stall.

❑ Not motivated to prospect. $_____

❑ Showing up for appointments and the $_____
   prospect is not there or not available.

Go back over the prospecting technique issues and check the three that are the most prevalent and really damaging to your ability to prospect. In the ($_____) space at the end of the statements you circled, write in the dollar amount this problem is costing you in commission income over the course of a year.

Add up the three numbers you placed in the ($_____) spaces and place the total here

These technique problems are costing me $ [   ] in residual income per year!

Did you realize how much these problems were costing you? How does it make you feel? Upset? Good. You should be very upset! You should take the time to feel how bad it's going to be for you if you don't fix these issues. Go ahead. Sit in it for a while. Now instead of being depressed you should get angry with yourself. Anger is usually more useful than despair! A little anger at yourself should help to engage your ego. Ego is what drives you to get out there and prospect.

The Cornerstone of Selling

Now that we've identified your issues with belief systems and techniques, let's look at my comprehensive model for prospecting. I call it the Cornerstone of Selling. The Cornerstone embodies a holistic approach that is much more complete than just teaching you a bunch of one-liners or glitzy "closes" that you'll never remember. It's much more solid than giving you a bunch of emotional stories about winning or people who have overcome some physical or emotional challenges. I'm all about developing you into a "solid" salesperson. When you have "mastered" the 4 areas in my Cornerstone you will exude a magnetic and strong personal presence that will draw people to you – and they won't even know why they are attracted to you! Here's what the Cornerstone looks like:

Belief Systems   **Strategy**

Techniques   **Activity**

Belief Systems vs. Techniques: A Symbiotic Relationship

Let's look at the symbiotic relationship between supportive Belief Systems and good Technique. If I had to choose between the two, as a Network Marketer, I would rather focus on identifying my non-supportive Belief Systems and replacing them with supportive ones over working on Technique. When you see yourself as strong and solid, there is no prospect in the world that can shake you with any objection or negativity. As I said before, when you have a strong sense of WHO you are and what you believe in the technique will just flow.

Obviously, having a good Strategy and knowing what you will and won't do to get an appointment is a very important piece of the Cornerstone in this example as well. But the moral of the story is that you can get by on little or no Technique when your Belief Systems about yourself and your opportunity are strong. I wouldn't ignore Technique though! Developing good Technique reinforces your Beliefs and makes them even more powerful.

Becoming proficient at Technique requires serious commit-ment. As I said in the introduction, you have to be willing to risk, fail and ask for help. You only "master" technique through repetition. The great news is when one of your "techniques" actually works (and you get over the shock that it did work!) it makes your Belief Systems ten times stronger and you become unshakable and **UNSTOP-PABLE** when prospecting. So having supportive Beliefs gives you the strength to execute Technique. And when you use good Technique and it works, your Beliefs are strengthened!

Chapter 3: You're Not In The Business You Think You Are In

What Business Are You In?

If I have a hundred Network Marketers in a room and ask them what business they're in, what do you think their answers would be? What would your answer be? Let's look at how the answers typically progress when I ask the question, "So, What business are you in?"

"The _____business" (insert actual company name)

"The Network-Marketing Business"

"Showing people how to stream goods and services through the Internet Business"

"The Duplication of your own efforts business"

"The Multi-Level marketing business"

"Network of Independent Business Owners that moves

products from Manufacturers to Consumers via the Internet"

"The Wealth Creation Business"

And finally some smart person with an excited grin that thinks they figured out the right answer (usually someone who has been to a Tom Hopkins Seminar) says,

"The People Business"

Not bad answers, but I'm about to introduce you to a concept some of you are not going to like. Some of you are going to hate it, but we need to deal with it up front and get it out of the way. If you are in the Network Marketing business promoting your Network Marketing concept:

YOU ARE IN THE PROSPECTING BUSINESS!

Ok, that's it. I've done it. The cat's out of the bag. I've said it. I'm sorry, but somebody had to do it! And if someone didn't tell you this up front, I apologize for them, but it's a fact and you're going to have to accept it and get okay with it.

Now some of you are a little shocked because you thought you got into a business of moving products or services through a Network Marketing business model and helping people realize their dreams. Some of you are totally missing this right now because you are saying to yourself, "Oh I know that already. I know I have to prospect. I do it!" In fact, you don't. You think you do, but let's put that Belief on the shelf for a minute. Let's discuss it and come back to it, then you can tell me if you really knew you were in the prospecting business.

Many Network Marketers get extremely confused about this issue. When they first get in the business there is a lot to learn, and much of it is very exciting. They start to learn about dreaming, commitment, selling, teaching, products, use of the internet, standing orders, showing the business, contacting, booking appointments etc, etc. In the course of their day they spend an incredible amount of well-intentioned time doing many of these things. Don't get me wrong. Listening to CD's, going to opportunity meetings, talking to your upline, using the products, directing people to web sites is all important stuff but it gives you the illusion you are building YOUR business. At the end of the day you "feel" like you have worked hard at your business. You drop into bed tired and satisfied having moved in the direction of your dream. But the fact is, unless you put someone new on your list or called someone to make an appointment, you actually faked yourself out and you did nothing to move your business forward!

You have started a business where the "it" all starts and ends with your ability to put people on a list, call them, and get them to meet with you face to face.

So I'm going to give you a set of rules. A rule defined by Webster is: *A fixed principle that determines conduct, behavior or habit.* I know from training thousands of salespeople that you won't be able to remember certain phrases, words or techniques from this book or from my CD's… especially when the pressure is on. But you will be able to remember the **RULES** and it will help guide you in your conduct, behavior and habit.

Network Marketing Contacting Rules:

Rule #1 - You Are In The Prospecting Business! Accept It And Don't Ever Forget It.

I recently did a seminar for a good client of mine who is a very successful sales manager for a financial services company. He asked me to talk to his brand new agents in training about prospecting. He had about 20 new recruits, all eager and ready to sell financial products. After I had spent about 45 minutes discussing my philosophies about prospecting I asked the trainees if they had come into this business thinking that they would be doing anything but prospecting. I said it was okay if they decided to quit now knowing this crucial piece of information. On cue the sales manager got up, opened the training room door, repeated my message and apologized to the newbies if he had not been clear about the prospecting side of the business. He said that anyone who didn't know what they had gotten into should feel free to leave right now with no hard feelings or questions asked. No one had the guts to get up in front of the group. The next morning three trainees resigned!

You may feel this was harsh treatment but we were actually doing these folks a favor. I'm not suggesting you should immediately quit your Network Marketing business if you're not totally ready to prospect. But you need to understand that to have fast and continued success-at ANY level- this is the business life you must know you have chosen. Which brings us to Network Marketing Contacting Rule number two.

Rule # 2 – **You Must Get Face-To-Face With A Steady Stream Of Qualified Prospects. Once You Have Developed This Ability, There Is Nothing That Can Stop You From Being Successful!**

This is the most important skill you can develop to assure your success in your business, or in the entire profession of selling. Once you can get face to face with decision-makers you can write your own ticket. I've interviewed thousands of salespeople for my own companies and clients. I have seen people who could close deals, present professionally, bond with people, look beautiful, know their product and work hard. They could sell, "brass knuckles to Gandhi" or "sell sand to Saddam" but if they can't, won't or don't know how to get in front of decision makers we don't need them!

I would take one good prospector over ten "closers" any day! This is great news for those of you who don't like to sell or don't think you are good at it! You don't have to be! If you can learn the skill of getting face to face with qualified prospects you can be the worst salesperson in America (and Canada). It doesn't matter how poorly you show the business, whether you can bond, or whether you look good or even smell good! If you have the ability to get in front of decision-makers, you've developed an extremely marketable skill that makes you very valuable to ANY company interested in increasing their sales.

Rule # 3 – **You Must Commit To Getting This Area Of Your Business Handled And "Master" The Art Of Contacting And Booking Appointments By Phone.**

Millions of people have entered the Network Marketing industry only to ignore this rule. They decide they need to learn about the products and get conviction and belief in them. They feel they need to learn the business before they will show it to anyone. They think they need to get good at showing the opportunity or they need to be able to confidently explain the compensation structure. They learn **EVERYTHING** except how to fill their list and how to get people to meet with them. **And they have failed!**

Let's look at the word commitment. What does that mean? Webster's simplest definition is: a pledge or promise to do something; dedication to a long-term course of action. Who are you making this promise to? You are good at making promises to your spouse, your kids and your employers. How about a promise to yourself? If you have reconciled yourself with Rule #1 and Rule # 2 (and you thought we were done with Belief Systems!), then it only makes sense that you must choose to go after this one with a vengeance until you've got it.

How about the word "mastery?" Webster says: ascendancy or victory in struggle or competition; masterly ability; expert skill or knowledge. Mastery is an almost outdated and lost concept. One hundred years ago a person strived to Master his/her craft, to become known as the best in their field. They were rewarded with money, but more importantly were given the respect of their peers and the community. The kind of respect you can only command after years of repetition and seemingly unrewarded dedication. I'm going to challenge you to Master this "art" because once you "own" it, it can never be taken away from you. I also guarantee that if you develop this skill you will gain the respect of your peers: the other successful, high-level Distributors that you aspire to be. Think about that for a minute and let it sink in.

What Kind Of Network Marketer Are You?

There are essentially ONLY three kinds of Network Marketers as it relates to prospecting. As we enter into this discussion I want you to be ready to answer two questions: Which one are you? And which one should you be?

The Farmer: A farmer by definition plants the seeds and then nurtures them until they grow into crops that can be harvested. No rocket science, here, but how does this analogy relate to prospecting? Most Network Marketers and salespeople take this approach. They'll tell you they get meetings and sell things (get people in the business) by building relationships. They are "relationship builders." When I interview potential salespeople and ask them why they think they'd be good at sales they tell me, "I'm a people person. I like people and know how to build relationships." We will go more into detail on the tragedy of this belief, but for our purposes this IS the way they sell. Now what does this mean? A "Farmer" prospector plants "seeds." They send people to web sites. They invite people to open meetings. They bait people with a piece of literature or tell a story about how they are succeeding or know someone who is succeeding in their Network Marketing opportunity. They stop by and see someone they know and talk about frustrations with jobs or income. They might even approach someone about the business and if they're told "no" they put this person on a list and keep in touch with them by sending articles or newsletters. They also show people their opportunity and follow up with them for weeks or months.

Can this approach work? The answer is yes. It is important to "plant" these kinds of "seeds." What is the intrinsic problem with "farming"? You have to wait for the

22

crop to come up and that takes time! If you have brought someone into the business and it takes a long time for them to sponsor someone, what is going to happen to their belief level? It's going to go down. From a business-building perspective the worst thing you can do to a new Network Marketer is to teach them farming techniques in the beginning because it takes too long to get results that way.

The Sharecropper: So what is a sharecropper in terms of prospecting? Webster defines a sharecropper as some-one who rents land from the landlord farmer and pays a portion of their crop as rent. A Network Marketer who sub-scribes to the sharecropper method likes to have the leads handed to them. They usually are very effective at getting other people to set up the appointments for them. In the general sales world these are salespeople who rely on their company to supply them with leads or appointments. I can't tell you the number of times salespeople with whom I've worked have told me that they could sell more if the company would only hire telemarketers to set up their appointments for them. Yeah, no kidding! That's what everyone wants.

A Network Marketer who is good at this usually can get someone in their down-line to book the appointments. Then the up-line comes in, shows the business and gets the prospect in. This is an incredibly effective way to build depth and create a lot of up flow excitement through a support team. The danger for the up-line sponsor is that they are not self-sufficient, and building width usually tends to be a big problem for them.

The Hunter: What does a hunter do? They can leave in the morning, go out into the "field" and come home with

dinner that night. The Hunter is completely self-sufficient. They can create business out of literally nothing. They have what I call a built-in "prospecting consciousness." Everywhere they go they see opportunities to add prospects to their list. When they are shopping, working at their day job, socializing, taking kids to events, recreating, playing sports, worshipping etc. They are in constant prospecting mode. This is the person who sees a bulletin board in a deli with business cards on it and picks them off thinking she'll just call them and ask them if they're happy in their career and making all the money they want to make. This is the person who gets an email from some-one requesting information about something work-related and thinks, "I'm going to see if they keep their options open as it relates to money making opportunities." This is the person who has a way to get the cable guy or telemar-keters home phone number! This is the person who walks off a plane with the business card of the person to the right of them and the person to the left of them. (Hunters always ask for a middle seat!)

The Hunter doesn't want anyone to book appointments for him/her or to take leads from the company's mailings or web sites. They know those leads are suspect at best. They would rather drive to show the business to people they have personally evaluated and qualified. When their list of friends, relatives and neighbors is exhausted they get excited and think, "Now, I can go find some prospects that will really listen to me!"

Farmer, Sharecropper, Hunter – Which one should you be?

So who are YOU? Did you relate with one particular style? Don't get too nervous at this point because the correct answer is that you should be ALL three. They all have value. Each "way of being" can work and allows you to have a good mix of prospects.

As a Farmer you definitely can get business by planting seeds. Keeping in touch with people who aren't ready to get in is a good strategy. Never burn the bridge with these people. When they do come around and are ready, it's like a bluebird flying in your window! That's a great gift – just don't count on it to reach the highest levels in your business in 18 months!

Sharecropping works too. Any lead someone is willing to give you-even if it's not hot-is worth following up on. If you're building depth down one of your legs, it's critical to get your downline to book the appointments. It makes them self-sufficient and gets you in front of their people. Especially if your new distributors are unable to show the business with skill and conviction.

Hunter Mentality Is The Key

Let's not kid ourselves here. If you had a psychic ability to determine ahead of time whether a prospect was a Farmer, Hunter or Sharecropper, who would you prospect? Who would you call and drive out to see? Yeah, me too! In a sales organization the Hunters are the most revered and valuable people to management or the owners. As a matter of fact in a small business the main Hunter is usually the owner! What a surprise! Hunters never have to worry about employment. They have a specialized skill that will feed them and their family well for a lifetime. The good news is that you can "master" a Hunter mentality. That's what this book is all about.

it. You start to believe they don't like you! You actually
e something deep down inside you that says, "They
't want to play with me. They don't like me. I'm bad!"

This sounds like playground stuff, but it's very real.
en you're making your initial list you're just putting con-
s on a list. That's all. That's why you need to put
ryone down that you know to start. Make your list
e. Have fun seeing ALL the people you have touched
r the years. At the same time don't try to decide for
m or care whether they would get in or not. Before we
o another contacting Rule let's review the three we
ady have:

**e # 1 – You Are In The Prospecting Business!
ept It And Don't Ever Forget It.**

**e # 2 – You Must Get Face To Face With A Steady
eam Of Qualified Prospects. Once You Have
eloped This Ability There Is Nothing That Can Stop
From Being Successful!**

**e # 3 – You Must Commit To Getting This Area Of
r Business Handled And "Master" The Art Of
tacting And Booking Appointments By Phone.**

Rule number 4 will give you incredible freedom to fill
list with **EVERYONE** you know. And if you're not
tionally invested in whether they get in or not you
't be emotionally crushed if they don't!

e # 4 – Stop Predicting And Start Approaching.

While we are on the subject of making an initial list let's
uss a few things about your closest friends, neighbors,

The Tragic Flaws of Network Marketers

Do you remember studying Greek Mythology in
school? You'll recall that Greek heroes suffered from the
concept of the "tragic flaw." This flaw was the one place
where they were vulnerable to attack – the place where
they were weak and could be beaten. One hero most people remember is Achilles. Achilles derived his super
human warrior strength from the magical waters of the
River Styx. He was dipped into the water as a baby by a
priestess who held him by the tendon on one of his ankles
– the one place the water didn't touch. Of course Paris'
arrow struck that exact tendon causing the death of
Achilles. Hence the term: Achilles tendon.

Well, Network Marketers have a number of tragic flaws
when it comes to putting people on a list, calling them and
booking a meeting with them.

Network Marketer Tragic Flaw # 1- They Believe That They Can Psychically Predict That Someone Will Be Good For The Business And Whether They Would Be Interested Or Not.

Most of the people that you revere at the highest levels
in your business would pay big bucks to learn this skill.
You think I'm being ridiculous, but in fact I'm dead serious.
You may miss this one because it's so automatic and so
ingrained you have what psychiatrists call a blind spot. Do
you know the first thing many Network Marketers do when
they start to make a list? They start to say to their sponsor or spouse, "You know who would be really good at this
business, Joannie and Todd. She's so nice and personable and Todd's a great salesperson." Hello Houston, we
have a problem!

This is bad, bad, bad! I'm sorry to be so eloquent here, but let's look at some statistical facts:

36% of all people have given up on having a better life and don't believe they will ever have more than a 5% increase in their income each year. They have had all the ambition beaten out them, accept their lot in life, and will defend it to the death.

10% of all people are lazy. They don't like to work and try to do as little as possible just to get by.

17% of all people will look at an opportunity just to prove it wrong and make themselves feel better that they were right!

3% have tried a network marketing business and "failed." They know "those businesses just don't work."

4% of the people make over $250,000 per year and feel that they are doing, "Okay"

What this means is that 70% of the people you will approach are not going to be seriously looking for something, and wouldn't even believe it if they saw something good.

So that leaves us with 30% of the population being potentially qualified to be able to "hear" and "see" a business opportunity as good as the one you represent.

You may think this is a depressing statistic but in reality it is an unbelievably liberating fact!

When you try to predict someone you know will be

great in the business, you set yourself up in a matter how great you "think" they are going t are they are not going to be ready. Do you s am going with this?

If you want to be successful in your Netw business you have to understand that many you put on your initial list aren't going to be in can do a great job approaching them, be exc showing the opportunity and do an awesome You can do everything right and it just won't they're "ready." Here's some more good new everything wrong and it won't matter either. S thing to do is to just go and do it!

This doesn't mean you should be pessim people on your list. You absolutely must thin hold the vision that they will get in. You must them and show the business believing they v to change their own lives.

Let's look at what happens when you put Todd (your next successful downline leg) on ALL these hopes and expectations. If they s take it personally. What does taking it perso mean? It means you then think it was about start to feel like there is something wrong wit they didn't get in because they don't think yo ful enough to begin with. Or you think you d of approaching them. You second guess you you should have waited until you were able t business better or you should have given it r gotten to a higher level so you could show th cess. You think it's because they don't respe ion and don't think you know a good busines

see
hav
dor

Wh
tac
eve
hug
ove
the
go
alre

Rul
Ac

Rul
Str
Dev
You

Rul
You
Cor

you
emc
wor

Rul

disc

relatives and work associates. This list is both an opportunity and a potential Achilles heel for you. These folks have the potential of being very excited for you and may see what you see in your opportunity. They also have the power (if you let them have it) to do some damage to your belief about the business. Many of your friends would not be excited if you succeeded beyond your wildest dreams – and theirs!

Why Your Friends and Relatives Don't Necessarily Want You To Succeed

You must realize that one of the greatest satisfactions some people have in life is being right about something. I love what one motivational speaker says about these people, "Don't stay away from negative people – run away from them!" The fact is: for many folks there is no greater feeling than being right. I have seen this syndrome many times in the sales organizations I train. A particular salesperson will develop a belief that there is no one left to sell in their territory or a competitor has a better price and will always steal the customer from him/her. They decide at the beginning of the year, "You can't sell this product in this marketplace anymore. I'll be lucky to break even with my numbers from last year." They start off believing they can't succeed and what do they spend ALL year trying to prove? That they were right! They are having a bad year and for all the reasons they thought!

Now if you are that salesperson, what do you do if you want to REALLY be right? You find some other salesperson and start telling them the company is doing the salespeople wrong and you drag them down with you so they have a bad year too! Now if they have bad year as well, guess what? You were really right!

Unfortunately many of your closest friends, relatives, neighbors and people you work with operate on a similar principle. If you don't believe this try this exercise: Sit down and think about some business idea you have dreamed about or thought you wanted to start. (80% of people surveyed have thought about going into business for themselves.) Flesh out a few ideas on paper. Make sure your idea doesn't have anything to do with moving products in a similar way to your Network Marketing business. Write down the basic idea, how much it will cost you to start it, how much you think you can make etc. Now go to ten friends or people you work with. In casual conversation while at lunch or visiting, mention your idea to go into business for yourself to them. Speak about it very seriously, as if you are really going to do it. Don't even ask them what they think. Record with secret amusement what they say. Compare your records of the ten conversations. What did you find? I know what you will find. I recently did this with about 20 friends with a business that I was going to start that was unrelated to my training business. To a person, the first thing out of their mouths was a statement about how it was going to be very hard to be successful. Some of them came flat out and said it was a good idea but they didn't see how it would work! They asked me all kinds of very negative questions insinuating that it couldn't work.

So why should mentioning your Network Marketing opportunity be any different? It isn't. It's about you wanting to try to make more money and develop a better lifestyle for yourself and that threatens a lot of the people you know. Which brings us to Network Marketing Contacting Rule number 5:

Rule # 5 – Your Friends, Relatives, Neighbors And Work Associates Provide A Valuable Service By Testing You!

The derision of your friends and relatives is extremely valuable because it's tests your conviction and belief and makes you stronger. Not only your belief in YOUR new business but also in yourself! Your closest people in your inner circle are always eager to tell you that something won't work! They are the experts on these things. God forbid they should say, "Hey go for it Joe! You're a hard worker; you're a sharp person, and if you think it's good I know you can do it. It doesn't matter what it is. I support you!"

When you're ready to approach the people closest to you, it's extremely important to remember Rule # 5. Anyone who speaks negatively to you about it will actually strengthen you and make your resolve and conviction deeper. Expect the test! I always smile internally when a prospect tests me. I see it as fun. So should you.

You're More Excited Than You Have Ever Been About Your New Business – And That's A Problem!

Getting into your Network Marketing business has energized you. You are excited about your dreams and goals and you see a dynamic vehicle to help you attain them. You believe you're on the ground floor of the next "mega trend." You have hope about having control over money and your choices. You SHOULD be excited, but this can also equate into contacting disaster! This brings us to Tragic Flaw number two:

<u>Network Marketer Tragic Flaw # 2</u> – They Believe That Their Excitement And Enthusiasm Will Rub Off On Their Prospect And Cause Them To Be Excited To See The Opportunity With An Open Mind!

I want to be crystal clear here. Your excitement and passion for your business is critical to getting people into the business, but not in the prospecting phase!

A sure-fire way to turn your prospects off is to be excited when you are approaching them. Think about this for a second. If we went out on the street with a video camera and a microphone and interviewed people and asked them to tell us what comes to mind when we say the words, "Network Marketing Person" or "Multi-level Marketing Person" what would we hear?:

Pushy

Hounds people

Too Darn Happy!

Cultish

Vitamins

Amway

Magnets

Herbs

Door to Door

Won't talk about anything else.

Always going to meetings at night and on weekends.

Never shuts up about it.

Never stops smiling.

Weird

Always trying to get you into something.

Always pitching something.

Listens to CDs all the time.

And of course they are EXCITED!

Is this what we would hear? Of course it is! Why? Because most people over the age of 25 have been approached at least once, if not 3 to 5 times, by some network marketing person. All of these companies train their people basically the same way, and they all come on strong with excitement, passion and enthusiasm during the prospecting phase. Prospects have come to recognize the pattern. When this "excitement" approach is used on them it trips their internal "multi-level marketing alarm bell" at about 100 decibels! They can see, hear, feel and smell a network marketing opportunity in the first 15 seconds of your phone call and usually wipe you out with about 30 seconds of questions. So that's why you need Network Marketing Contacting Rule number 6:

Rule # 6 – Never Show Excitement Or Enthusiasm When Contacting Or Booking An Appointment – Save It For Your Seminar Or Opportunity Meeting!

Prospects are also experts at picking up on your language and use it to detect a "network-marketing pitch." Each network marketing company has its own techno-speak. Most of them use a number of generic terms that scream, "This is another network marketing business!" Which brings us to another Tragic Flaw:

<u>Network Marketer Tragic Flaw # 3</u> – They Use "Buzz Words" That Signal To Their Prospect This Is Network-Marketing

When making contacts or making phone calls to book an appointment, NEVER say the following words or phrases:

We're excited

My Wife (Husband) and I got into a business.

I want to show you an opportunity.

Home based.

Support Team

Up line

You need to see this.

You need to meet this guy/gal (they're really successful and super rich)

I want you to come to a meeting with me and meet some great people.

People I know have a meeting every month

Ground floor

Ground floor opportunity

<u>Rule # 7</u> – No Buzz Words!

I mean NEVER say them! Eradicate them from your vocabulary! The only place for your buzzwords is your local seminar or meetings with fellow Network Marketers. Even then, be careful because talking like that can spill over into your prospecting language.

There is a corollary rule to Rules 6 and 7. This rule solidifies these two rules. It gives the underlying reason why you should adhere to 6 and 7 and shows the potential problem if you violate them

Rule # 8 – If You Want To Be Treated Like All The Other Network Marketers, Walk, Talk And Smell Like All The Other Network Marketers!

How do Network-Marketing people get treated? Poorly would be a nice way to say it. Like pariahs would be more accurate. Like crap would be to use the vernacular! The minute a person detects you are involved in network-marketing, they relate to their previous experience with network-marketing people… and usually it's a negative experience. Displaying ANY of the characteristics of a network-marketing person will guarantee challenges to your cold contacting or your phone call to set up a meeting. At the very least you are going to get questions, objections and stalls that are going to be very tough to handle. At the worst, your prospect is going to unload all their venom against network-marketers on you. It will seriously shake you if your belief is not strong. Stop acting like a network-marketing person. Cut it out! Got it?

Eventually, you're going to reach the point where you're going to run out of names on your personal list. For some it will happen rather quickly depending on how many people they have met in their life. It's possible that you have moved to a new area and don't know many people. Whatever the reason, you need to reach out to people you don't know in order to fill your list. I refer to this prospecting activity as Cold Contacting. You can call it Warm Contacting or Gold Contacting if it makes you feel better, but I call it this to distinguish it from approaching or contacting people you know.

Let's review the Network Marketing Contacting Rules:

Rule# 1 – **You Are In The Prospecting Business! Accept It And Don't Ever Forget It!**

Rule # 2 – **You Must Get Face-To-Face With A Steady Stream Of Qualified Prospects. Once You Have Developed This Ability, There Is Nothing That Can Stop You From Being Successful!**

Rule # 3 – **You Must Commit To Getting This Area Of Your Business Handled And "Master" The Art of Contacting And Booking Appointments By Phone.**

Rule # 4 – **Stop Predicting And Start Approaching.**

Rule # 5 – **Your Friends, Relatives, Neighbors And Work Associates Provide A Valuable Service By Testing You!**

Rule # 6 – **Never Show Excitement Or Enthusiasm When Contacting Or Booking An Appointment – Save It For The Seminar Or Opportunity Meeting!**

Rule # 7 – **No Buzz Words!**

Rule # 8 – **If You Want To Be Treated Like All The Other Network Marketers, Walk, Talk And Smell Like All The Other Network Marketers!**

These Rules will serve us well as we prepare to Cold Contact. You will use many of the principles in these Rules to guide you. There is an additional set of Rules that are very specific to Cold Contacting because this kind of Contacting has to be done in such a "Ninja-like" way. The reason it has to be done with some finesse is because approaching someone to show them a business opportunity has an inherent problem: You are reaching out to THEM. This is the opposite of what they find in their world and so some people are automatically suspicious and their defenses come up a little. If you aren't careful, they will start to sniff around to see if they can smell a network-marketing approach.

Let's review Rule # 4 and the context around it:

<u>Rule # 4</u> - Stop Predicting and Start Approaching.

Remember we said that only about 30% of the population is conceptually ready to hear about a business as good as your opportunity? Using my numbers, that leaves 84 million people still left to prospect who are qualified to see your business. I want you to focus on the incredible freedom this gives you. This means that 70% of the people you meet, say hello to, or even get a phone number from may not be ready. So it doesn't matter if they say, "NO" to you at any point. You can now meet people all day long knowing it doesn't matter if they like you, want to give you their number, talk to you again or think you are a stalker! Who cares if they say "NO" when 70% won't get in anyway! It's like you could say to someone, "Would you be interested in finding out about a business opportunity where you could make unlimited income and not have to work?" They say "No," and you say, "I didn't think so," and keep right on moving! So, this brings us to an important rule to help solidify your contacting of people you know as well as Cold Contacting. Network Marketing Contacting Rule number 9:

<u>Rule # 9</u> – People Want Things They Can't Have!

Again, the inherent problem with Cold Contacting is you are reaching out to them, and they're just not used to it. The mistake many Network Marketers make is they send signals showing they NEED this person to talk to them or get on their list. When prospects sense you NEED them, they will smell it faster than a Doberman smells fear! If they sense any kind of need or your "wanting them to get into something" they will put their defenses up and start ripping your face off with some pretty hard questions! Now if that happens, who cares – right? No matter how strong you are, let's use some good technique to avoid this.

Chapter 4: The Power Of The Interviewer: Maintaining Strong Posture That Attracts People To You

We can learn a lot from the way people approach a job search and the way the interviewer handles the interaction. Let's look at the hoops an interviewer will put a job applicant through to get a feel for the way you should be "acting" when you are meeting and contacting people.

Step One: The Interviewer places an ad announcing a job opening. The applicants are told up-front they must possess certain qualifications to be considered at all.

Step Two: Applicants are told to forward resumes to a PO Box or an e-mail address. Applicants send their job histories into space hoping to be noticed among all the other candidates.

Step Three: The Interviewer or secretary calls and tells applicants they have qualified to come in and interview with the Interviewer. When applicants have some questions, they are put off by the Interviewer and told they will have a chance to ask questions in the interview.

Step Four: Our eager applicants dress up, spruce up and show up on time for the interview. Why? They were taught to make a good impression.

Step Five: Our Interviewer makes the applicants wait for 20 minutes and then ushers them into the interview room. They survey the resume, frown and start asking questions. They ask questions that make applicants feel like they're on the spot. Each applicant does his/her best to answer the questions, giving what they feel will be the best answer. Interviewers try to trap the applicant by asking derisive questions like, "Why did you leave your last job," with a tone that is like, "Prove to me there is a good reason here."

Step Six: When the interviewer finishes, they don't give any indication to how well the applicants did or if there will even be a next step. Applicants are then told, "Well, we have a lot of resumes to go through and some more people to interview. If we don't get back to you in a week or two will you call us?" Even though our applicants have just been put through the ringer, they smile and thank the Interviewer for treating them like second-class citizens and hope they get the call for a second interview.

So Who Is In Control Here?

Don't miss this because it's powerful stuff. We've all been through some version of this process. Can you believe the garbage people go through to interview for a job? Most jobs aren't even that good, yet people jump through ALL kinds of hoops to even be considered. Let's look at some of the reasons our Interviewer is able to maintain such a strong and intimidating posture.

Posture Is Everything

Interviewers are powerful because they choose to be! They set up the rules of the game and the applicant follows. The Interviewer knows they have something the applicant wants, and dangle it like a juicy steak just out of the dog's reach. The Interviewer unconsciously uses human nature to his/her advantage. Human beings want things they can't have and will always struggle to get them. If you want to raise this desire to an insatiable pitch, just tell them they have to compete against other humans for the thing they can't have. This makes them crazy and willing to do anything to beat other challengers... even if the prize stinks! If you then make the "prize" very difficult to obtain, it increases in value exponentially. Look at what people go through to apply for a job! It's degrading! And yet they do it all the time! Competing to win a job they know they won't like.

You Need to Maintain This Posture When Contacting

Your prospect gets tough with you and starts asking questions like, "Is this a pyramid?" or "Tell me exactly how the business works and then I'll see if I'm interested to meet with you", when your posture is weak. They "smell" when you need them. They smell it like a dog can smell fear, and just like a dog, they go on the attack!

So you must get rid of your neediness. Stop picturing them as your next successful downline team. Stop letting your eyes light up with that excited eager look you get when you meet someone sharp and say to yourself, **"Oh boy, they'd be great in this business. I can smell my 4% bonus check for life!"** You need to have the body language, the voice inflection and eye contact that says, **"I don't care if you are interested and you probably won't qualify anyway, but I'm going to do you a favor (maybe) and allow you a chance to get a glimpse of the greatest business in the free world if you don't screw it up!"**

When contacting, it is critical for you to be nonchalant. It should seem like it is not that important for you to get their card or number. It almost has to seem like it was an after thought on your part, and that you are doing them a favor by suggesting you might want to contact them. When you own this belief system, the "technique" will just flow out of you automatically. You'll be amazed how you won't even care if they ask you a tough question. And you won't care if you answer it or not! Now that's power, and that's what makes a great cold-contactor! Let's look at some techniques to reinforce your belief system for the heck of it.

Techniques, Strategies And Activity: Turning Your Belief Systems Into Actions.

In this section I'm going to teach you the specific techniques and skills you will need to contact people you meet and how to book a appointment with them that is solid.

Chapter 5: Cold Contacting: Ninja-like Methods To Add To Your Prospect List

The Mechanics Of Making Contacts

There are some very distinct stages of Contacting that you need to be aware of. They look like this:

1. Initial Contact.

2. Observation Comment

3. Name Exchange

4. Reason for Information

5. Set up the Re-Contact

We will now launch into specific behaviors and techniques you should pay attention to. As always, your Belief Systems will drive this kind of behavior and technique in you anyway. Let's continue on with some more Rules that will explain the stages and what to do in each.

Rule # 10 – Every Person You Meet In The Course Of Your Day Deserves To Know What You Know.

If you've developed the Hunter mentality and have a prospecting consciousness, every person you meet should be given a chance to see the opportunity. Remember Rule # 4 – No predicting. At this stage everyone you meet is a prospect if they have the ability to fog up a mirror!

44

Rule # 11 – You Do Not Have To Get The Name and Number Of Everyone You Meet – Just Get Good At Meeting People!

God forbid we should smile at people, be pleasant and say hello! What a concept. Especially where I live in the Northeast where we could definitely use a little more friendliness. In the first stage, "Initial Contact" is simply making eye contact and then a nod of acknowledgement perhaps with a slight smile. Not grinning-idiot stuff or cultish-like happiness. If you are really stoked, tone it down a little. Just be confidently pleasant, make eye contact and acknowledge you are both sharing the same space and you will connect.

Rule # 12 – Be Observant And Look For An Opening Statement To Start A Conversation – You Can Always Say Something To Get A Person To Respond To You.

I want you to try an exercise that will change your Belief System about meeting new people. For 3 days straight, I want you to meet people without caring or trying to get their names or numbers. Just start with a slight smile and a form of hello. Then follow up with a comment about something you're observing about the environment you are sharing with them or something you observe about them. If you want to have some real fun try it when you are riding an elevator. I love a captive audience. I did the elevator exercise recently and here are some examples:

In a hotel a man got on counting change in his hand. I said, "That's not going to buy you much in this restaurant." He said, "I'm looking for the floor with the soda machine. Do you know what floor it's on?" We started talking.

An attractive young lady got on the hotel elevator carrying some legal pads and a laptop computer. Her back was to me. I leaned forward, nodded to the items in her hand and said, "What do you sell?" She said, "Pharmaceuticals to OBGYN's." I said, "That's easy." We talked about how difficult it was to have a doctor set an appointment with her and she said, "What do you do?" I said, "I'm a consultant. I help people meet people on elevators." The whole elevator laughed. I got her card and the name of her sales manager.

A young man dressed casually got onto an elevator in a building. I saw him come out of an office that said "Product Ventures" on the door, to get into the elevator.

I nodded to him and said, "Do you work there?"

He said: "Yes."

I said: "What does the company do?"

He said: "Product Design."

I said: "Big Company?"

He said: "About 30 people."

I said: "Who's the owner?"

He said: "David Johnsen."

I said: "Good guy to work for?"

He said: "Yeah, he's okay I guess." We got to the ground floor. We started at the 4th.

I said: "Take it easy."

He said: "Stay dry," because it was raining, and I got another name of a business owner for my list!

Three women walked on one at a time as the elevator went down three consecutive floors. I waited until the third one got on and said, "Boy this elevator is smelling better and better each time we go to the next floor" Everyone laughed and the women who did not know each other started a lively conversation amongst themselves. I just listened and enjoyed the fragrance.

You don't need to be a comedian, but a lighthearted approach can be helpful. Just say hello to people. You must have some kind of an "Observation Comment" to get things started. How many times have you waited for the other person to take the initiative and were relieved when they did it? Just say something. Some people will be cold and won't respond. Who cares! That's their problem. The best part of Cold Contacting is you get to have some fun and enjoy yourself.

Rule # 13 – Your Goal When Contacting Is To Get A Name, An E-mail address Or Number And A Reason To Call Them – That's It!

This is not the time to start asking someone about their dreams or even their dissatisfaction with their job. You do not want to start qualifying them now. You do not want to get into a conversation about what you do, your side business, or any of that. Focus on learning how to go from the "Observation Comment" to the "Name Exchange" first.

Rule # 14 – Get their Name – It Helps When Contacting Them!

After you make an "Observation Comment" they will usually answer or a conversation will ensue. If this is a person you have never met there is usually a "Pregnant Pause" where you are either going to keep it on a casual level and just make initial comments to each other or take your "relationship" to the next level. You are now about to enter the complicated "Name Exchange" phase. At the pause (somewhat uncomfortable) **I always say, "By the way, I'm Mike Durkin"** and I reach my hand out if it is a man. If it is a woman I may just nod and smile as I say, **"By the way, I'm Mike Durkin"** If they have not received the script you may need to use what I call a Sentence Finisher and say, **"And you are..............?"** You have great conversations with people you meet in all kinds of circumstances and then walk away never exchanging names. You meet them over and over again at your kid's practice and never introduce yourself. Shame on you. Stop that. It is difficult to go to the "Reason For Information" stage if you don't know their name.

Rule # 15 – Your Job Is To Get Information Not Give It – You Are Under No Obligation To Answer Any Of Their Questions!

The way you stay in control is to make sure you are the one asking the questions. Conceptually, Belief System-wise you must be strong and maintain the "Interviewer's Posture." If they have questions for you, you will answer them when YOU want to. There are certain psychological reasons you feel you have to answer their questions, but you don't! If you are interviewing for a job, and you ask a question that an Interviewer doesn't want to answer, do they stop and make a big deal of it? No, they either ignore

48

your question or tell you they will get to that later. Do you stand up and say, "Either you answer my question or I'm out of here!" Of course you don't. You patiently wait for an answer that sometimes never comes! In my next book I'll give you my sure-fire formula for staying in control using questions.

Rule # 16 – Do Not Allow Yourself To Be Cornered – Start The "Reason For Info." Stage Just As You Feel The Interaction Is Getting Ready To End.

It is important for you not to launch into the "Reason" stage too early. This stage is the "reason" you need their information. If you do it too early, you risk all kinds of questions and things that you don't want to get into. Remember when you go into the "Reason" stage you must not be excited, needy or enthusiastic. You must maintain that nonchalant posture an Interviewer would have when asking for this information. There are a number of "reasons" you can come up with, and you are limited only by your own creativity. Let's look at a couple of approaches:

I often let the interaction end, even shaking hands with the person and saying goodbye to them. I'll then turn and use the old "Colombo Hand on the Doorknob" approach and say, **"By the way, do you have an email address?"** They will say, "Yes." I reach into my pocket and pull out a pen and someone else's business card and say, **"Write down your email address on the back of this card. I may have something I want to get back to you on."** As they are writing the email down I say, **"Why don't you throw your phone number on there, too."** They hand me the card and I'll say, **"It was nice meeting you. I'll get back to you but it won't be right away, so you'll have to be patient"**

If they try to ask a question, I say firmly and with good eye contact, **"I don't have time to get into it now, I'll be in touch in a week or so. Is that okay?"** They'll say, "Sure," Now, get the heck out of there!

If they say they don't have an email address, you say, **"Do you have electricity?"** This always gets a laugh and then I say **"Just write your phone number down. I'm working on a few deals with some partners and it might make sense for us to talk sometime."**

Why is the "Colombo" approach so effective? When you turn to leave, all your prospect's defenses are down. They think it's over and you are out of their life forever. When you turn and say, "By the way…" you catch them a little off guard and there is less chance of being cornered and nailed to the wall by them.

You must be very assumptive and solid when you come up with the "Reason for Info." It can be anything you want it to be. The key is to keep it simple… don't feel you really need to explain anything. It's good to have a rehearsed answer about what it is or what you do, but you don't have to explain it. As a matter of fact, the more mysterious you are about it the more people will be interested. People won't ask you questions if they feel they will be jeopardizing you getting back to them to tell them what it's about. I give the impression (with my attitude, I don't actually say this) that to ask for more would be inappropriate at this stage. If they really push me I'll say, **"Well, I'd have to check with my partners to see if I should even be talking to anyone else at the moment. Besides I couldn't promise you anything. So let me get back to you. That makes sense, doesn't it?"**

Another method to help you in the Reason for Info stage is to write up an article or two that discuss "Wealth Creation" or use some ideas from your upline discussing the power of duplication. Create the document in Word and make it look like an article. Having these articles written and available by email now gives you a ready-made excuse to get their card or email address. **"By the way, do you have email? Write your address down here and I'll send you some articles my partners wrote on using the Internet to make money. Why don't you throw your phone number on there in case I need to get back to you."**

I have a number of articles that I've written and I ask people for their cards ALL the time so I can "send them an article I've written." I get at least an email address 95% of the time!

Rule #17 – **Have A Rehearsed Answer That Describes Your Business And What You Do But Don't Be Too Enamored With It!**

The problem with a really cool or mysterious answer about your business is that someone may start asking you questions that you really don't want to get into in a face-to-face contacting situation. This would be my personal favorite: They ask you, "What kind of business is it? Or "What do you do?" I would reply, **"Let me answer your question with a question. Have you ever thought to yourself, 'Boy, there's all these people making money selling products and services using the Internet and I wish I could figure out how to cash in on that?"** They will say some version of "Yes" to which I say simply, **"I have some partners with whom I help people with business ideas market them using the Internet. That's**

what we do." If they ask more questions like how do you do it or how does it work, they've just given me the "Reason for Info" and I then say, **"Do you have an email address? Write it down for me and I'll get back to you with some info. By the way write your phone number down too."**

<u>Rule # 18</u> – Never Give Them YOUR Business Card – Always Be Out Of Them So That You Have To Ask Them For Theirs.

I know you want to be professional and business-like, but it makes you too anxious to give your cards out if you have them on you. Some of you whip that card out like a black belt throwing a ninja-star...whoosh! All of sudden it appears in your right hand faster than Siegfried and Roy could get it out! Aggressively handing out your business card sends the message that you were there to do that – and prospects start to suspect you have an agenda. If I do decide to give them a card I say, **"I probably gave my last one out. I never have them on me. Maybe I can find one. Do you have one? Does it have your email on it?"**

Chapter 6: **When To Make Your Calls or Head Games Network Marketers Play To Avoid Making Calls**

One of the common questions I get in my seminars is, "When is the best time to call a prospect?" I then ask a question in return, "So when do you think is the best time to call? How do you determine your calling times?" I always have an internal smile when I ask this because I know my trainee is about to reveal his/her "head trash" about prospecting to the whole room. Here is a sampling of statements I have heard salespeople make about calling businesspeople at work:

"I always wait until 10:00am to call because I know how busy I am when I first get in the office. So I let things calm down for my prospect first."

"I never call on Mondays because people are just getting back from the weekend and they're not ready to receive sales calls. I like to give them time to settle in."

"I don't like to call between 11:30am and 2:00pm. That's when most people are either thinking about lunch or at lunch and I'm just wasting my time leaving voice mails."

"I don't like to call right after lunch because people are usually tired after eating and that's not the best time to approach them."

"I never make calls on Fridays because people just aren't into working on Fridays and their head just isn't into it."

"Forget calling in the afternoon in the summer. You can't get anybody to pick up the phone."

"Most business people are too busy in the morning with meetings and planning. I call in the afternoons."

"I'd love to call earlier than 9:00am but most switchboards aren't open and I'll just be wasting my time."

"I like to call early, before 9:00am, get through the

switchboard and find people in their offices. Then they can concentrate."

"During the summer, forget calling on Fridays and Mondays."

"People are not into it after lunch. I never make calls after lunch."

"I try to get all my calls in before 3:00pm because nobody wants to get a sales call when they are thinking of going home."

"In this business forget calling people during the holidays. There's a moratorium on making decisions."

Well, I hate to tell you but it gets worse when you're talking about running a home-based business and want to call people at home. Let's look at what I've heard from Network Marketers about calling prospects at home:

"You can't call people between 5:00pm and 8:00pm. That's dinnertime and you'll interrupt them. They'll be upset and that's no way to start a prospecting call."

"I never call right after work. People need time to shake off the day. I call between 7:00pm and 9:00pm."

"I hate it when my phone rings at home, at night. It's usually some telemarketer. I'd rather call people at their business."

"Sunday night is the best night to make my calls to book appointments. People are home and preparing for the week."

"I would never call on a Sunday night. It's still the weekend. That's rude."

"I can't imagine calling on a Saturday or a Sunday. The prospect would think that was weird to get a call about a business opportunity on a weekend."

"It's a waste of my time to call on a weeknight. No one is ever home. All I get is voice mail."

"By the time people get the kids to bed it's after 9:30pm and you can't call that late, you'll upset people."

"Every time a telemarketer calls it's during dinner. I hate to be interrupted during dinner. I hate the idea of interrupting someone's dinner."

"Someone told me that the best nights to call are Tuesdays and Thursdays. People work out on Monday nights and they go to church or school meetings on Wednesdays."

"You can't reach people during the summer. It's a waste of time. I'll call right after Labor Day."

The list can go on and on and on. The more my trainees talk the more embarrassed they become. It becomes excruciatingly obvious to everyone in the room that you can play whatever mind game you want with yourself. It's not unusual for any type of salesperson to try to psychically predict the optimum conditions for making an appointment or making a sale. I can remember as a rookie salesman trying to decide if I should call on my prospects on rainy days because I was convinced that they would not be in a good mood and I would blow my one good chance!

So what's the answer here? You can't predict the success of your call. You can call a prospect in the middle of burning the dinner or one who's relaxed sipping coffee saying, "I wonder if there's a business I could start that has little overhead and great upside residual income built into it?" You don't know so here's my high-tech, Harvard business school, triple MBA advice: Call. Just CALL for goodness sake! Who cares when? Remember the statistics: 70% are not ready! It doesn't matter WHEN you call them. It just matters that you call them! Pick up your prospect list and just CALL!

Cell phones make it easy to call at ALL different times and give you an excuse to say, "I'm on my cell driving, I need to make this quick................."

Call when:

You are driving to work in the morning.

You are driving home from work in the evening.

You are waiting in a waiting room for an appointment.

You are in the parking lot at work before you go into work.

You get home from work between 5:00pm and 9:30pm.

You are on your lunch hour.

You have just finished dinner.

The kids are asleep.

The kids are awake.

The house is quiet.

The house is noisy.

You are making dinner.

You are cleaning the garage.

You are sitting in your office "making calls between 7:00pm and 9:00pm."

You are rushing off to work in the morning from your house.

You are driving to the hardware store on a Saturday morning.

You are waiting for the kids to get off the bus.

You are making breakfast on a Sunday morning and you sneak off to your office to make one quick call.

It's Sunday night and everyone is home from 6:00pm till 9:30pm.

You are sitting in your car waiting for someone to show up for some kind of appointment.

Etc., Etc,...

It doesn't have to be perfect. I have never made a

perfect prospecting call in my life. As a matter of fact, the more nonchalant I was about it and the more I didn't care how I did it, the better the call! Just CALL! If you get good at putting people on a list you need to get just as good at getting them OFF the list!

Most Network Marketers just need to start making the calls. You will probably screw some of them up. Who cares? Next! Call. Call. Call. And call some more!

Chapter 7: Scripts: Why You Should Have One And How To Use It

I have heard all kinds of belief systems over the years about what to say on a prospecting call and how to say it. One of the things that kills a Network Marketer quicker than anything is having a couple of bad calls where they stumbled over their words or got tongue tied and embarrassed.

So I always suggest having a script. I get all kinds of resistance and hear things like, "I can't read from a script, it's not me. It's not natural" or "I hate it when telemarketers call and you can tell they're reading from a script."

In the absence of a script, MOST Network Marketers **WILL** get tongue tied and screw up (while they are being natural) and it will become so painful to make a call they will do most anything to avoid making calls anymore! So please don't tell me you can't read a script!

It is important to use a script for a number of reasons, and there is a right way to use a script-and a wrong way. Let's cover some ways and some reasons:

58

1. Having a script gives you a starting place, a springboard. The toughest part of any call is the beginning. It's launching into the first couple of lines. Once you get started in most cases prospects will go along to some degree and the call usually gets a little easier and more natural because prospects participate (even if they are negative or suspicious).

2. Having a script allows you to get back on track. As I told you in the last chapter, I have never made a perfect call. That's true because you can never predict the crazy things prospects may bring up or the direction the call can take. I've launched into my first couple of lines only to have the prospect cut me off and start telling me their life story! There are many times when prospects take you in a direction you never expected. I guarantee you if you don't have a script, you are never going to get back to booking the appointment and you'll be stuck answering a lot of questions you do NOT want to get into.

3. Having a script gives you confidence. Real or not, it doesn't matter. My script is always my lifeline no matter how strange the call gets. If you've made calls you know what I mean! No matter how tough your prospect gets, no matter how tough an objection they throw at you, you can always look down at the script and just read. Sometimes the script helps you "plant your feet" and stumble through. Often, the prospect accidentally goes along with what you are proposing! Imagine that. Left to your own devices you will falter and default to letting the prospect off the hook because it's the

easier thing to do. Just knowing the words are there if you need them makes you stronger.

Rehearsal – Should you practice your call to the dog or in front of the mirror?

I've heard ALL kinds of different rehearsal techniques over the years from all types of trainers that have probably never made the call they are suggesting you make. I'm not denying that reading your script out loud a few times to your spouse can help get you comfortable with it, but let's not kid ourselves. The best way is to get in the trenches and make some calls. Screw up! Make some mistakes! Look foolish! It's okay. This isn't heart surgery... it's a sales call. You'll live if they say NO! You'll live if they think you're CRAZY! You're going to get NO's! Feel this: NO! NO! NO! NO! Still breathing? Still have your 401K money in your account? Still going to have a baked potato with your steak tonight? You'll be FINE!

The point is you should not wait until you have it perfect before you start calling. Just call. Calling can be your rehearsal, and you will learn a lot and have a lot of FUN doing it. Imagine you were calling trying to get "NO's"! How fun would that be? "Hey Honey, I just hit my goal for the night. I got 10 "NO's" Let's take the kids out for ice cream!"

Audio Acting – Making your script sound as if you're not reading from a script.

All of us have the propensity to "sound " as if we are reading it, when we read from a script. I would suggest you use a technique I call audio acting. Try this exercise:

Call up a few friends on the phone and have a portable cassette recorder with you. Record your side of the conversation and play it back later. What you will notice is that in "normal" conversation you "screw up" quite naturally. There's plenty of pauses, "Um's", "Ah's" and "Yups" When having a normal conversation people will sigh, breath, pause, increase volume, speed up, slow down, gasp etc.

When you read a script, you have a tendency to strip out all the "normal" parts of a conversation. So I suggest you add them back in! When reading the script you need to do some "audio acting" This means purposely pausing, slowing down and throwing in a couple of "Ah's" and "Um's" This makes you sound more realistic and more believable. Can you imagine how much fun you can have when you are reading from your script and you are purposely NOT trying to sound professional. Try it. It works!

Don't you dare "ad-lib" or you'll destroy your call.

Only kidding! "Ad-libbing" is perfectly acceptable and makes your call more natural. I never use the exact same words every time I call unless they are real critical phrases that can get the appointment booked. Use your script as a template or a guide. You'll probably say it a little differently every time, but it's good to have ALL the words there just in case you need them.

Chapter 8: Tips For Staying Motivated: How To Sound Strong And Confident On The Phone

Posture and Physiology – Is yours helping or hurting your calls?

Try this exercise: Sit at the desk or table you usually

make your prospecting calls from. Now, position yourself so your eyes are looking down at the floor or at least down at the surface of your desk. Keeping your head down, lean forward and let your shoulders sort of slump down. Come on now, humor me! Scrunch your stomach over and breathe as shallow as you can. Now, think very negative, depressing thoughts. Come on, stay with me! Think of all kinds of horrible things like train wrecks or the terrible poverty in all parts of the world. Think of as many depressing things as you can. Now, if you are right-handed, pick up your right hand as if bringing a phone to your ear and stop. If you are left-handed pick up your left hand as if bringing it to your ear and stop. Hold this position for a minute. Does this remind you of anyone? Is this the position you end up in while making your calls?

Is it any wonder that after making 5 or 10 calls like this you lose energy? Does it surprise you that after making 10 or 12 calls like this you start to get negative about the calls and about yourself? It shouldn't! If you have assumed this physiology when you make your calls, you have assumed the posture that millions of salespeople take everyday. You have also assumed the exact physiology that behavioral psychologists have observed in severely clinically depressed individuals. Some studies have shown it is actually the depressed posture that somehow activates the depression.

This is not the kind of state of mind you want to be in when you are making prospecting calls!!!

Try this exercise: Stand up, quickly and energetically. Take some deep breaths. Breathe deeply and fully from your diaphragm. No really, do it. Think about some really positive things like how much money you can make if you get just a few good people into the business with you. Think about all the good things being done in the world to help people. Now, look up with your eyes toward the ceiling. Keep your head straight, but just look up with your eyes. Keeping your eyes looking up try to frown. Just try it. You can't do it, can you?

By changing your physiology you have changed your "state" and have put yourself into a powerful and confident place to make calls from.

How a headset can improve the effectiveness of your calls.

One of the best contacting investments is to purchase a headset that is wireless or has a cord long enough for you to stand up and walk around. Standing frees your diaphragm and allows you to breathe with purpose. The ability to stand and walk around while making calls will energize you and will radically improve the quality of your phone calls.

Try making two or three calls sitting down with your usual posture. Now, stand up using the headset and make two or three calls. See how it feels. Notice the difference? Most of my clients report they instantly feel more powerful or at least have the ability to be more forceful. Now try making a few calls and walk around while you do it. Start picturing your prospect as if they were in front of you in the room and you are talking to them live. Try adding some hand gestures, again as if speaking to them live or trying to make some points to get through to them. By "walking and talking" you will actually change the resonance and persuasiveness in your voice. I can't tell you scientifically if anything changes in your vocal chords, but I do know for a fact you will project more presence and charisma on the phone.

Grab your prospect by the throat in a nurturing way!

You've got to make an impression on your prospect and "come across the phone" in a way that is going to grab their attention. Not in an excited, off-the-wall kind of way, but in a way that makes you sound different from all the other mundane calls they receive in the course of a day. Your prospects are bombarded with communications of all kinds: Voice mails, cell phones, work phones, home phones, pagers, e-mails, etc. If you sound the same as every other call they receive, you are going to be treated like every other call they receive...you are going to get blown off! By standing up, walking around and "acting" a little bit you will project a presence they will not be able to ignore. Again, I don't want you to sound urgent or needy. I want you to sound confident, powerful and in control of this call. Remember what I said in a previous chapter: People want to do business with people who are solid. They want to be around people who can energize them and bring some value to their lives. They will pick up on your presence over the phone and will find themselves saying "Yes" to you and not even know why they gave you the consideration after ducking dozens of other sales calls. Believe me. Practice "walking and talking" and don't worry if you look foolish to anyone who walks by and thinks you are a crazy person having a conversation with someone who isn't there. Hundreds of my clients have confirmed that purchasing a headset and "walking and talking" has completely turned their prospecting around 180 degrees. Trust me on this one...it works!

Chapter 9: Using Your Ears To Hear: How To Develop Instant Rapport Over The Phone

Using the phone to make your appointments and book your meetings has some obvious logistical conveniences, but it has one inherent problem. The phone call itself is auditory and relies on both parties' auditory abilities and skills. Since you can't see your prospect's facial expressions and other body language, you have to rely one hundred percent on what you are delivering verbally. This means you are going to have to listen, and therein lies the problem because most people are not good natural listeners.

Using your ears to hear and your mind to listen– You can learn everything you need to know about your prospect over the phone.

Your prospect will give you a tremendous amount of information about themselves, their current state and how they are receiving your information with a number of very obvious clues; if you are ready to hear them!

Most of us, however, are used to relying heavily on our visual senses to read how we are coming across and how people are reacting to us. This is one of the reasons people will say, "I hate the phone" or "I'd rather talk to someone in person rather than on the phone." It doesn't change the fact that the phone (even with the advent of voice mail…which is a total pain in the butt!) is still the most efficient way for us to reach prospects and book appointments. Here are some tips for listening and how to use what you hear to your advantage:

1. Listen for ALL the things that are happening

in the background of the call.

The instant your prospect picks up the phone you need to have the ears of a kit fox! Listen for sounds that let you know what is going on in their environment at that very moment. If you really listen you can pick up on how receptive they will be based on the situation going on around your prospect. Listen for sounds of kids playing, dinner being cooked, dinner being eaten, children screaming, arguments going on, TV's blaring or the deafening sound of quiet! If you are calling your prospect at work listen for the sounds of machinery running, switchboards ringing off the hook, paging systems blaring out your prospects name or your prospect's co-workers talking or yelling to them. Be aware of what you are hearing and what it says about your prospect in the moment.

2. Get into their world quickly.

One of the ways to bond with your prospect instantly is to get into their world right away. Remember that THEY interrupted their world by picking up the phone. They chose to pick up the phone but what ever is going on for them is probably still going on –and that's not your fault or problem. How many times have you been interrupted at home by a telemarketer who ignored your screaming child and just continued to read their script? How did it make YOU feel? You were just annoyed or bored because that telemarketer did not take into account anything that was going on with YOU. They were totally "I" centered and gave you no reason to engage with them and bring them into your world.

When you hear things going on in the background it gives you a great opportunity to connect with your prospect. For example if your prospect answers the phone and you hear them holding a child wailing at over 100 decibels you could say, "Wow. Sounds like things are pretty busy there right now. I know when my kids are like that I can't even handle picking up the phone. You're pretty brave to do it" or "How do you do it?" I guarantee you that you are about to hear a story from them about their 5 kids and how they learned a long time ago how to answer the phone when things are crazy. In addition, you will have bonded with them and shown them you are not "I" centered. You will have communicated that you care, or at least recognize what is going on for THEM. They will sense that you are not just concerned with what YOU wanted to talk with them about.

I am not looking for you to have some huge bonding conversation here. I just want you to acknowledge something you hear that allows you to empathize with what is going on for them, that's all. I'll go into more detail in the chapter on making calls.

3. Listen for tonality – It can tell you everything.

This next form of listening is going to take some work for most of you but you all have the ability to do it and do it well. This is the art of understanding your prospect's tone to know where they are and "who" they are. When you listen for your prospect's tone you listen on a deeper level because you are using your instincts to translate what you hear in the tone of their voice. It reminds me of Obi-Wan-Kenobi telling Skywalker in Star Wars, "Search your feelings, Luke!"

Well, in most cases, I would tell you that your "feelings" won't really serve you in sales. But in this case they are essential and you are going to have to access them!

Your prospect can communicate truckloads of information to you just by the way they say, "Hello" when they pick up the phone. In my office when I answer the phone myself, I usually dispense with hello and answer, "MJ Durkin!" Now, I have several versions of "MJ Durkin" and my voice changes in tone, pitch, speed and volume every time I answer depending on my mood, my environment and what is going on in the present for me. Here are just several translated versions:

"MJ Durkin!" short, clipped and fast, which means: I've got a proposal to do, I'm under the gun and I'm late for my next appointment.

"MJ Durkin" relaxed, slow and easy which means: "I've got an easy day today, all my work is up to date and I'm open to whatever anyone is going to say to me on the phone"

"MJ Durkin!" tight, curt and gruff which means: "Something or someone just ticked me off and God help you if you are a salesperson with a bad or boring pitch because I need somewhere to vent and I'm sooooooo glad you just called!"

"MJ Durkin" light, happy and lilting which means:

68

"I just made a huge sale, it's Friday afternoon, work is done and I'm open to anything you have to say or sell even if it's stocks in the next up and coming ostrich farm in Texas!"

So you can see that even though the words are exactly the same every time, my tone will communicate to the caller everything they need to know – if they are using their ears to hear and are actually listening!

So what do you do with this information? It's important reconnaissance and you may do absolutely nothing with it. Be aware of whatever you can read about them. If you sense you have caught someone at an incredibly bad time, I would suggest you put that on the table and say, "Sounds like I caught you right in the middle of something. Should I call another time?" Again, search your feelings and follow your instincts. It may be totally appropriate to make a comment about your prospect's mood or situation and it may not. The rule here would be if you hear something that is very over-the-top, you probably should mention it. For example: Let's suppose your prospect answers with an unmistakable, gruff and angry voice. They are apparently NOT trying to hide it from you so at some level they want you to know they are angry. They could hide the fact from us if they wanted to. (All of us have experienced our psycho parents yelling at us when we were kids and then picking up the phone right in the middle of getting ready to deliver the death blow to us and saying in a sweet, lilting voice, "Helloooooooooo?")

So our prospect is communicating to us in a very strong way and if we ignore it, we would actually be showing them we are not sensitive to what is going on. We would be remiss if we DIDN'T mention it. In this case I might say, "Sounds like today isn't a good day. Should I call another time?" Or "It sounds like you're having the kind of day I was having yesterday. I was in no mood to talk. Should I call back?

Most people will appreciate you taking the time to be empathetic with them. They will either share what they need to say to clear the air or they will realize they need to make a shift. If they don't dump on you they might say, "Oh no, it's okay. Why were you calling?" Either way, you have acknowledged what was going on for them and at some level bonded with them and developed a bit of rapport with them.

How to use the information you've gathered to create a deeper level of rapport

Since you are limited by the auditory nature of your call, you have to find a way to create rapport without the use of facial expressions, body language and eye contact. So you are going to have to use your voice to make a connection with your prospect. This is actually a very powerful tool that can make your call extremely effective.

In order to use your voice as a bonding "weapon" it is important to understand how people bond with each other. I'll give it to you in the form of a rule.

Rule: People like people that are like themselves.

This is one of those of those trite phrases that you will miss because you will have a tendency to say to yourself, "Well, MJ that's not a profound secret. Try telling me something I don't know."

While in fact it is simple, thousands of salespeople violate it everyday by being unique individuals who think that they are special. They try to stand out and show how different they are. Many salespeople have been taught to differentiate themselves from the competition and they think that this applies to their personality and bonding. Making a phone call to book an appointment is NOT the time to shock someone with your ability to be a diverse and unique individual.

People join the Republican Party because they want to associate with Republicans. They join the Democratic Party because they want to be with Democrats. Stamp collectors join the stamp club because they want to be around other philatelists and cave explorers join the cave exploring club because they want to hang with other spelunkers.

For all of our talk about the advantages of diversity when it comes down to it most people like people that are like them.

Now on a phone call I don't want you to try to bond with someone by finding out that you both have the same political beliefs or that you both like exploring caves! But you have an incredible opportunity to use your "new found ears" to develop a level of rapport that will increase the effectiveness of your calls by about 30%. The techniques I will teach you next are so powerful that your prospect will never know why they felt so comfortable with you on the phone and why they blew off every other network-marketing person except you!

Matching and Mirroring – Tonality, pitch, volume and speed

When you make your initial phone call and you are "using your ears to hear" you will notice that your prospect has a unique way of speaking. As we've discussed whatever is going on in the moment may be affecting whether or not they are speaking fast or slow or loud or softly. (Depending on whether the chicken is burning or the kid is biting them in the leg) In addition to what may be going on in their environment or with them in the moment, each individual has their own unique style of speaking.

Now, you can either get in sync with their "style" or you can continue to use your "unique style" because you have one too! For example, our local Chamber of Commerce president is a man named Steve who has a very deep, resonant voice. He speaks very deliberately, calmly and slowly. I on the other hand have a rather high pitched and forceful voice. I usually speak very quickly and somewhat excitedly. Steve usually takes his time to get to a point and I usually drive fast to the bottom line. When I call the Chamber I tend to be myself and say with enthusiasm, excitement and speed, "Hi Steve! It's MJ Durkin! How are you today?" Steve will reply slowly, deliberately and deeply, "Hello MJ. How are you?"

Now, I can continue to be me, MJ, and keep speaking at my high pitched accelerated pace and be a unique individual with my own speaking style. But what is happening for Steve? I am so different from Steve in the way that I speak I may actually annoy him. Have you ever had someone's voice that was very high-pitched and so different from you that it was like fingernails on a chalkboard to you? Or someone who spoke so slowly and deliberately that you were like, "Come on, come on already. Get to the point!" At the very least Steve is going to have a hard time feeling comfortable with me because I am so different from him. Most of this stuff happens on a very subconscious level and Steve may hang up the phone and think, "Gee, that MJ's not a bad guy but there's just something about him that rubs me the wrong way."

So what is the answer? The answer is to "match" my speaking style so that it is more in sync with his. Now you have to be careful because you can't imitate someone's voice because they will think that you are mocking them! In the case of "Excited MJ" and "Resonant Steve" the best thing that I can do is to slow the pace down a little bit. I can take some of that high-pitched nasally stuff that's in my voice and make it a little more resonant. And it's easy of course to just speak a little softer.

Remember that people like people that are like themselves. When you get on the phone and start listening to your prospect the first thing you want to make sure of is that you don't create dis-rapport! Now that's not a word but it's important to not do anything that will hurt the bonding. At the very least if you notice that your tonality, pitch, volume and speed are different from your prospect don't accentuate your differences. You should slowly try to match your prospect. If your prospect is a fast, loud, high-pitched talker and you are much slower just raise it up a notch or two. As they speak some more and you get a feel for how they sound and the tempo they use you can raise it up another notch. Again don't go over the top. I'm from the Northeast and when I call down to the Southern states there is obviously a big difference in our accents. When my prospect answers with that lilting Southern drawl and says, "Hi Mr. Durkin. How ya'll doing up theeeere in CT?" I don't drawl back imitating saying, "We're all fine up heeeeere. How ya'll doing down theeeere?" But I will guarantee you that I will slow down my fast and harsh

Northern way of speaking right away and by the end of a long conversation I'll even be throwing in a couple of "Y'alls" (without the drawl of course!)

Have you ever noticed if you go and visit another part of the country for any length of time that you will come back using phrases and maybe even a bit of their accent? You can't help it. People like people that are like them and people try to be like the people they are with. It's human nature.

Practice these techniques in low risk situations. Start listening to the calls that you make to friends and relatives and start listening to the differences in each ones' speaking style. Slowly start to "match" tonality, pitch, volume and speed and it will become second nature and you'll automatically do it on prospecting calls. I guarantee it will pay huge dividends.

Chapter 10: Why Network Marketers Are Inconsistent With Their Prospecting And How To Fix It

In my seminars I do an exercise by asking my trainees to write down the number of prospecting calls they think they should be making per day. For our purposes we will look at a 7-day week because calling people about a Network Marketing business can be done on the weekends as well. I then have the trainees share their numbers with the group. As a matter of fact, as an exercise you should do the same. Write down the number of calls you should make per day to book appointments to show your opportunity.

It's hysterical to me because when I ask the question I

see all kinds of consternation on their faces and the questions start coming. Do you mean the actual number of people you reach and talk to? Do you mean the number of people you will call and get a voice mail? Do you mean the number of people that you will book an appointment with? Do you mean the number of people that you get through your script and actually talk about the business to and ask them if they will meet with you?

Let's look at my original question: Write down the number of calls you should make per day to book appointments to show the business. Why is this so difficult? Because Network Marketers that don't want to make calls want to make the formulas as complicated as they can because they are looking for excuses not to make the calls. They immediately start to make it difficult.

Let's keep it simple, assume that it's my fault and I'll ask a more direct question using some old fashioned terminology to make it very specific. How many dials can you commit to making every day to book appointments to show the business? (Even though most of us never actually dial anymore!) Don't worry about reaching people, voice mails or basically getting anyone live.

So you've written down a number of dials you can commit to making on a daily basis. (You decide if you are working off of a 5 or 7 day week) In my seminars I then ask everyone to shout out the number that they write down. In 90% of the cases the numbers that are shouted out are just downright crazy! They are numbers that people "wish" they could commit to but they really can't. They'll say things like 10, 20 or 30 a day. For the most part the numbers are totally unrealistic. Let's put these numbers aside for a moment.

Why most Network Marketers won't get to the number they committed to.

Let's look at what happens to a typical Network Marketer's prospecting schedule. Our well-meaning Network Marketer looks at their calendar and sees that on Monday night they don't have any appointments to show the business so it's a good night to fill their calendar.

Monday

They decide that they will get home at 6:00pm, have dinner and make calls from 7:00pm till 9:30pm. It's a good plan. All is going well until after dinner and they get out their list and their calendar. But what happens? Just as they are getting ready to call their phone rings and it's a friend who has a problem and needs to talk. That takes about 25 minutes but they had to help their friend. Our Network Marketer now settles back down to call again and what happens? Their 5-year-old son comes running in screaming that their brother just smacked them in the face with the dog. That takes another half an hour to settle down and keep everyone from killing each other. It's 8:00pm now and as they get ready to call again they get an instant message on their computer from one of their downline asking some questions about products. They go back and forth on the internet for a while and then decide to turn it into a phone call. That ends and it's now 8:30pm. After all this hard work our Network Marketer now decides they are kind of tired and finds their way into the kitchen. As they are taking a "well deserved break" their spouse comes home with enough groceries to feed a whole battalion and of course they are enlisted to get the food at least into the kitchen. It's now 9:00pm. They are just getting ready to go into their office to sit down when the doorbell rings. It's their neighbor with a UPS package that was dropped off at the neighbor's house. The Network Marketer thanks the neighbor and they chat for a while updating each other on what's going on in the neighborhood. It's now 9:15pm and the Network Marketer looks at their watch and says, "It's too late to make calls. I'll make some tomorrow night" No calls made today.

Tuesday

Again our well-intentioned Network Marketer forgot that Tuesday night is out for making calls because there is a meeting at the school that will run till 9:00pm. No calls made today.

Wednesday

But don't worry because Wednesday night is free but as they sit down to make their phone calls at 7:00pm a relative calls with a crisis and they have to stay on the phone for most of the night consoling and taking care of this person. You can substitute everything here from: The car broke down and they didn't get home till late or they had to stay late at work. No calls made today.

Thursday

Our well meaning, committed Network Marketer knows that it's been a bad week for making calls but they are determined to sit at the phone for a good 3 hours and make up for lost time. They actually get to their desk at 7:00pm and just as they are getting ready to make their first call they hear their 12-year-old daughter crying in the next room. They go to check on the problem and the daughter informs them that she ruined the poster board she was doing her project on that it is due tomorrow. The daughter begs the Network Marketer to take her to the local stationary store before they close so she can get some more poster board. Well it's family first and they can't let the 12-year-old get a failing grade on the project. They get through traffic, wait in lines and get back around 9:00pm. The Network Marketer is so tired they say to themselves, "I'm in no shape to make calls now and besides that it's kind of late to start calling people." I'll call tomorrow. No calls made today.

Friday

It sounded good last night that they were going to call tomorrow but the Network Marketer forgot that today was Friday and of course you're going to be wasting your time to try and reach people on a Friday night. To ease their guilty conscience they decide to go out and get some pizza and play some miniature golf and tell themselves that they will cold contact some people while they are out. No calls made today.

Saturday

Saturday morning and possibly the afternoon sounded like good times to make some calls but the Network Marketer forgot that they had to go to their niece's christening and a party afterward. The day is shot for prospecting but they did meet two new people at the party so they feel like they worked on their business a little today. No calls made today.

Sunday

Our Network Marketer has some personal beliefs that

make Sunday a day where they wouldn't do any business and that's fine. They thought perhaps it might be okay to make a few calls Sunday night and catch a few people home before the week started. They were a little uneasy about calling on a Sunday night because they felt that people would still think it was the weekend and that it was weird that they were calling. They got a reprieve though. When they went to access their list the computer crashed and they had to spend the whole night fixing it. No calls made today.

This is not that unusual – Life continues to happen to you even after you get your Distributor ID Number!

So how many of you have had a week like this? How many of you have gone a whole week without making one phone call to book a meeting? How many of you have gone two weeks? Three?

Don't get me wrong. You could have been very active in your business with all kinds of other things related to the business. You could feel like and in fact have been working hard. But if you're in the prospecting business and you had week like this you are in big trouble because your calendar for the next week is going to be light with appointments to show your opportunity. There are number of factors at work against you here.

How your number of daily dials and your prospect list work against you.

Let's suppose you were one of those people who had a high daily number of dials. Imagine you had said you could make 20. (You usually set a goal like that after a particularly good seminar with an especially motivating speaker!) So you have great intentions but think about what this number of dials does to you? You've set a lofty goal because you've been taught to set the bar high. But if you can go a whole week without making even one call you're being unrealistic and your number starts to become a negative. If you don't have a daily goal perhaps you pull out your prospect list before you make calls. If you've put 50 or so names on your list it looks HUGE to you. It's great that you have a large list but you are going to get the feeling that you have to make all those calls in one sitting and that's going to sound and feel very heavy. Most people associate a huge amount of pain to the idea of sitting down and making a large number of calls or saying that they are going to make calls from 7:00pm till 9:30pm. So here's Network Marketing Contacting Rule # 19 –

Rule #19 - If You Associate Pain With Prospecting You Will Do Everything You Can To Avoid It!

I'm going to tell you that having a large number of calls to make each day or to block out a long period of time to make calls can become very daunting. And if you see the process as negative or painful you will ALLOW all of those interruptions to happen because you are secretly glad that they are happening! Every time you have a chance to do something other than sit down with your list and make the calls you will take it!

So how do you break this pattern? How do you make your goal a positive thing? How do you make your goal, your list and your block of prospecting time a motivator as opposed to a de-motivator?

Disclaimer: If you do not relate to having weeks like this and you when you sit down to make calls you

actually call for the three and half hours please skip the next chapter and go to directly to chapter twelve and also go directly to the highest level available in your company.

Setting an "Activity Goal"

In chapter one I showed you the "Cornerstone of Selling." One of the "corners" was Activity. Here is my definition:

Activity is the energy that you put forth making prospecting calls to book appointments.

Without Activity nothing happens in YOUR Network Marketing business. You can have every other part of the business down but if you don't have Activity and you don't do it consistently you will find that you will be extremely frustrated because your business just won't grow!

Let's go back to our example of the week from hell where every time you got ready to prospect you had "prospecting- interruptus." As we said, this is not that uncommon because life is still happening even though your goal is to have the kind of life reaching a high level in your business promises. One of the problems here is that you "set up" your pre-determined times when you are going to prospect and you count on them happening. When they don't happen you end up not prospecting at all.

I have worked with thousands of salespeople who have the same issues and they get paid a salary to prospect! It's a part of their job description. As a matter of fact, they are encouraged to block out entire 8-hour days to make calls and fill their calendars. But they never do it! The potential pain of making all those calls almost necessitates that they get involved in servicing their customers to have valid excuses for not getting to the calls. I have seen salespeople that will admit that they look for problems to solve to avoid prospecting. Some of them will actually admit that they create problems so that they can solve them and avoid calling prospects!

So what's the answer? I am about to divulge an incredibly powerful secret that will change your prospecting life forever but many of you will miss it. It is going to take a little bit of planning on your part and many of you are not going to be willing to do what it takes to make this strategy work. This next secret is for those of you who are really committed to succeeding in your particular business model. Some of you will see it's genius immediately and will begin to implement it right away but many of you won't.

How to set an Activity Goal and why it works!

1. You must set a goal that you can achieve on a **daily basis**. No more huge blocks of time to make calls. (You don't do them anyway!) The goal that you set will be the number of actual dials that you will make each day to call someone on your list and potentially book an appointment with them. So before you set your goal you need to see yourself being able to make these calls sometime during your day. As I described in chapter 9 it could be on your lunch hour, in the parking lot, in your car after work or in your office at home

2. The goal must be incredibly, almost ridiculously realistic. When most of you wrote down the daily number of dials you could make you shot to high.

Some of you said 10,20 or 30. Unless you're unemployed and have a lot of time on your hands those numbers are crazy for most of you. You won't do it. Some of you will actually fool yourself and believe that you do. So here's what the number actually needs to look like: It needs to be a number that you could commit to even if all that stuff we described during the prospecting week from hell happened. It has to be a number that you could hit even if you had a day from hell and your boss asked you to come in early and stay late. It has to be a number you could hit even if the kids were sick and you had to leave work and stay with them all day. It needs to be a number of dials that you said, **"No matter what happened in the course of a day I could commit to making those dials no matter what!"**

3. This means the number needs to small! You aren't going to be able make a large number of calls, every day 7 days out of the week. You just won't do it. Now everyone's schedule is different and some of us have more time than others. So I don't want to push you to set your goal too low but experience has shown me that most people set the goal too high and never reach it consistently. When they don't reach it consistently they realize that it was unrealistic and they usually stop trying altogether. The small number works and here's why:

The small number works because anyone can a do a little bit of something every day.

Let's assume for a minute that you set your Activity Goal for **3** per day. Doesn't sound very high does it? I mean anyone can make three calls per day can't they? I mean couldn't you squeeze one in during lunch? And you could certainly call someone before you left the office or from the parking lot at work couldn't you? And in between everything at home you could certainly make one call before 9:30pm at night couldn't you?

Well, you're thinking, "Sure MJ but that's just 3 dials per day. What if you don't get the person on the line? I could make 3 dials per day and not reach anyone!"

I agree so let's do the math. Let's suppose you make 3 calls per day, 7 days per week for 365 days a year. That's 1,092 calls per year! Now you might even say to me that the number still doesn't look like enough considering that you don't reach someone every time you dial. That's true. But I'd like you to take out whatever amazing electronic device that you have your prospect list stored in and count the number of prospects that you have on your list. Do you have 50? Do you have 100? Do I hear 150? Let's suppose that you have 100 people on your prospect list. Do you think that during the next year that if you make 1,092 calls at all various times of the day, 7 days a week that you will be able to reach ALL 100? I think you can and I think you will.

Let's extrapolate just a bit more: Let's suppose you have 30 Distributors in your downline. They all make just 3 dials per day. That's 32,760 calls per year. Do you think if your downline made 32,760 dials this year that something is going to happen in your business?

If 32,760 dials are made in your downline something IS going to happen. Even with bad technique something is going to happen! The key here is that every Network Marketer can do even a small amount of prospecting every day. I learned this from people in the 12 step programs who know that they have to deal with their addiction problems one day at a time. They know if they think of not drinking or drugging for the rest of their life it's too huge and it freaks them out. But anyone can NOT do something (like pick up a drink) for just one day, right?

There is magic in setting an easy, small, realistic number of dials **that you will make every day**. Even if the number is 1.

Consistency and associating pleasure with your calling can make a huge difference in your prospecting

If you are doing what most Network Marketers do you're trying to set up large blocks of time and trying to make large numbers of calls. This can cause you to go for one, two or even three weeks without making ANY calls. Look at the three-week results if you just make 3 easy dials per day. If you work off of a 7-day week you will have made 63 dials. That is a one hundred percent increase in calling over the three weeks where you made no calls. Of course the answer is that you need to commit to consistency when you set your Activity Goal. We will need some way to hold yourself accountable and also get some support in keeping you consistent. We'll deal with those issues in the next chapter.

Chapter 11: Tracking Your Prospecting And Holding Yourself Accountable

One of the big problems Network Marketers have is thinking that they are prospecting when in fact they aren't. They actually get in some form of denial because they keep themselves very busy with Network Marketing-like activities. They remind me of the hamster on the wheel. They feel very tired at the end of the day and even satisfied that they have worked on their Network Marketing business but they haven't done the most vital thing they need to do. Let's review a few Network Marketing Contacting rules:

Rule # 1 – You Are In The Prospecting Business! Accept It And Don't Ever Forget It.

Rule #2 – You Must Get Face To Face With A Steady Stream Of Qualified Prospects. Once You Have Developed This Ability There Is Nothing That Can Stop You From Being Successful!

Rule #3 – You Must Commit To Getting This Area Of Your Business Handled And "Master" The Art Of Contacting And Booking Appointments By Phone.

So you can see that everything else that you are doing to build YOUR business is just extraneous stuff. I'm not saying that it's not important but I don't want you to fool yourself into thinking you are going to hit the highest level in your business because you learned about a new product.

So we need a way that a Network Marketer can effectively track if they are in fact hitting the Activity Goal on a daily basis with consistency. To this end I invented the **"Activity Tracker"** The Activity Tracker is a very simple form that can help you track your calls and look at your consistency from week to week. If you go to the appendix at the back of the book you will find an example of an Activity Tracker.

Now I know with all of your fancy electronic devices and software that my Activity Tracker is going to seem a little archaic to you. But I want you to bear with me because even with the advent of Palm pilots and Act programs I find the same thing that I found 10 years ago with the salespeople that I train; which is very little prospecting going on no matter how sophisticated the device or software is! My rule is to keep it simple and putting hash marks on a piece of paper is about as simple as it gets!

Here's how the Activity Tracker works:

1. Take out an Activity Tracker and put your name on it. Your goal is to look at it every morning and reconnect with what your Activity Goal is and picture where and when you will make the calls you need to make to match your Activity Goal.

2. Fill in the date for the "Week of" i.e.: Week of July 11th.

3. In the space where it says "Activity Goal" write in the amount of dials that you can commit to making each day during the week.

4. On the corresponding day, put a hash mark down in the space that says, "# of dials" every time you dial the phone to make a prospecting call to set up a meeting.

5. If you have matched or exceeded your Activity Goal you can write in "10" in the space where it says, "Consistency Rating" for the corresponding day. If you have done less dials than the Activity goal try to give yourself a rating equal to the per-

centage that you've actually done. So if your goal was 4 and you only did 2 give yourself a 5. If your goal was 5 and you did 2 give yourself a four. If you've made NO calls that day give yourself a big fat "I'm going to be stuck in my job forever" 0.

Everything, Everything, Everything that you do around this Activity Tracker will reveal something to you about how you are as a Network Marketer and a person

By taking out the Activity Tracker every morning and looking at your Activity Goal you will know very clearly what you have to do. And if you have set the goal realistically it should be a fairly positive and reachable outcome. At the end of the first week you will start to see your pattern when it comes to prospecting. Remember, you will have some days where it seems very tough to make your Activity Goal but you committed so that's that. That means that by 10:00PM that night you might be making that last call to keep your commitment. But as you look at the pattern you will start to learn a lot about yourself.

Your actions will always tell you about the strength of your commitments

There are various things that you will notice about yourself "IF" you commit to working with the Activity Tracker. Here are just a few:

1. Some of you will love the idea of the Tracker and will say that you will do it but you will never pick it up. You'll never actually try it even though you are very motivated right now as you are reading this. You may have attended one of my seminars and stated, "I'm going to commit to using this for the 30

days. I call this person the **"Motivated Wisher."**

2. Some of you will use the Tracker sporadically. You'll remember it one day and then at the end of the next day you'll groan and say, "Oh no, I totally forgot about it! I'll do better tomorrow." You will use it the next day and then forget to take it to work with you. You'll miss two days and then you'll use it for two days. I call this person the **"Absent Minded Prospector."**

3. Some of you will use the Tracker for about two weeks and then you will lose interest. You may make your goal every day but if you don't get results right away after two weeks you'll decide that it doesn't work and that it's wasting your time. You'll actually make a conscious decision to stop doing the Tracker. I call this person the **"Doubting Prospector."**

4. Some of you will set an Activity Goal that is higher than most because you just can't see the value of setting the bar so low! You like to set lofty goals and impress yourself and others with goals that are in outer space so if everybody thinks they can do 3 a day you just know you can double that and set yours for 6. What you will find is that even though you look at the tracker and write down the Activity goal for each day that you very rarely match your Activity Goal with the # of dials. As a matter of fact, you never hit it and you are very glad you didn't hit it because you shot so high. But you'll notice some thing about setting a high goal. If you look at the Tracker each day, morning and night you'll notice that many days you don't make any dials. I call this

person the "**Over Achieving Prospector.**"

5. Some of you will say, "I've been looking for something like this to keep my prospecting on track." You will look at the Tracker day and night. You'll put a realistic Activity Goal in each day's space and you will do everything short of calling your relatives by the end of the day to match the dials with the goal. You will do the Tracker every day for 30 days. You'll carry it with you in your planner and have it with you in your car, at lunch and waiting for appointments. It will become a habit for you that is positive and you will start to see your calendar filling up with appointments to show the business. I call this person "**Diamond, Director, ENVP, RVP, Sr.VP etc...**"

Your actions around this Tracker will show you who you are "being" You will absolutely fall into one of these categories or some version thereof. The way you show up around the Tracker will be the way you show up around YOUR business. The use of (or lack of use) of the Tracker, spouting off big goals and then not following through at all or inconsistently using the Tracker will show you WHO you are. I will guarantee you that you are also showing up in life the same way! This will be a real scary exercise for some of you or it is really going to confirm for some of you WHO you are; and you're going to like who you are.

What if you want to or can make more calls that day than the Activity Goal?

If you can make more dials than the goal you set then that's great. Nothing succeeds like success and the best time to make a call is when you have just had a call that went well. If you make your "5" calls for the day and you have the time then call like crazy. Go ahead and do 50 calls! One way to get to a high level in your business fast is to do massive amounts of Activity! But the key here is that you **ALWAYS** do the minimum **EVERY DAY**. No more of this sitting down, making 20 calls and then doing nothing for a week. That doesn't work.

Holding yourself accountable

So you've gone two days and haven't even looked at the Tracker but who will know? Well, you will but even that may not be enough to keep you honest. I grant you that sometimes in the whirl of life you do forget. I suggest that you find a "buddy" in the business that is also using the Tracker. It can be someone in your upline, downline or crossline. You let your buddy know what your Activity Goal is and you find out what theirs is. I know many salespeople that have worked with this idea that will call each other by the end of the day to see if the other person made their Activity Goal. Some will immediately call their buddy when they have made it. If your buddy doesn't make their goal you question them and hold them to their commitment. And if they can't hit their goal consistently then you hold their feet to the fire. You tell them that they either set their goal too high of that they are "wind bagging" because their actions show that they really were not committed. Be tough on your buddy and expect them to be tough with you. You can set up whatever system works for you but some kind of daily contact with your buddy is essential. Again, only about 20% of you will actually pick up this system and run with it.

Managing The Numbers

Many of you have people in your downline that come to you for help. They say they are committed to growing THEIR Network Marketing business. They are willing to meet you at 2:00 am at the local diner if need be to get your counsel. That's great. I suggest you ask them to show you their Activity Tracker sheets for the last 30 days before you start "motivating" them. Remember that the Activity Trackers will be a clear indicator of who they are "being." Everything, Everything, Everything that they do around the Tracker will reveal to you who they are being as a Distributor in your business and as a person.

If you find any inconsistency around using the Tracker you need to ask some questions to find out the reasons for the inconsistent behavior. Your Distributor could perceive that they have a time issue or they might just be afraid to make the calls because they only have 15 people on their list. Asking questions around the use of the Tracker starts to help you pinpoint where the real issue is. It could be a Belief System issue, a Strategy issue, a Technique issue or an Activity issue. For example: if your Distributor whips out 30 or 60 days of Activity Trackers and they have made the dials but they aren't booking appointments then they probably have a technique issue. There is probably something going wrong in their telephone approach. If you look at their calendar and they are getting a sufficient number of meetings but prospects aren't getting in then they have some kind of problem with the type of people they are showing the business to. It could also be a technique issue as it relates to how they are showing the business.

In most cases you will find that your Distributor hasn't really done the Tracker consistently. Remember that I asked in a previous chapter, "Anyone can make just 3 calls per day, can't they? That's easy isn't it?" That's why when you ask to see the Tracker sheets for a month you will start to get all kinds of stalling and "the dog ate my homework" kind of stuff. You can't manage what you can't measure and if your Distributors can't fill in the Activity Tracker then they shouldn't be getting your valuable counseling time! Straightforward enough? You should hear me say it live. I'm not all that nurturing when I say it!

Chapter 12: What To Say When You Call Your Contacts And How To Book A Solid Appointment!

Rules And Observations About Booking Meetings

The main thing to remember when you are getting ready to call your cold contacts is the posture of the Interviewer. As the Interviewer you have all the power AND you have ALL the attitude. You have something that they want and need. You MAY give them a chance to get it. Let's look at Network Marketing Contacting Rule # 20:

Rule # 20 – You Are Under No Obligation To Answer ANY Of Their Questions And It Will Actually Hurt You If You Do!

Some sales courses spend all kinds of time teaching you how to handle objections. When making appointments they teach you one-liners to handle objections and they think that will give you confidence to make the call. That's garbage. Why not just be strong and have confidence without the one-liners! Imagine that you are the Interviewer when calling to invite someone to come in and interview for the job you have available. Your applicant starts asking one question after another about the job; how much it pays, what are the hours, what is the boss like etc. How would you act if you were the Interviewer? What would your attitude be? Would you as the Interviewer get nervous? Would you start thinking, "Oh no, they're not going to come in for the interview and I better sell them to come in or I'm going to lose them!" Would you answer their questions if you didn't want to or didn't feel they were appropriate to go into over the phone? NO! You wouldn't. As a matter of fact they would start to lose points with you and you would start to project an attitude of, "Hey wait a minute pal! Don't ask me to many questions or you might not qualify to come in and interview and by the way don't tick me off!" The more questions they asked and the more they tried to take control of the phone call would actually hurt them in your eyes and you would be giving them the impression that they don't qualify and you are going to dump them!

Interviewers Don't Care If You Like Them

Let's put you in the seat of the Interviewer again. If you are the Interviewer and your applicant doesn't like the way YOU are conducting yourself on this call do you really care? Are you as the Interviewer trying to be liked? Heck no! You are testing your applicant to see if they make it through the phone interview to make it to the next step. Good Interviewers don't try to make friends with you! They are doing a job and are actually listening very hard for ANY "attitude" on the part of the applicant so that they can flush them! If the applicant gives the Interviewer a hard time and doesn't want to come in for the interview does the Interviewer get all wounded and upset that the applicant didn't like them? What do they do? They cross that one off the list, say to themselves, "Well that saved me a bunch of time" and they **MOVE ON TO THE NEXT**

CANDIDATE WITHOUT BLINKING AN EYE!

Prospects Are Attracted To People That Are Solid

I know, I know. You want some technique. Enough of this belief system stuff, right? You need to get this now. It's not the magical phrases or the one-liners that get people to want to see you. It's your attitude. It's your posture. It's the fact that you don't feel that you have to answer their questions. That's what attracts them to you and makes them feel like they would be missing something if they don't meet with you. When you project this aura of conviction and belief, that you have something they need and want and you MIGHT give them a chance at it, technique isn't even necessary!

The Mechanics Of The Call

1. Reminder

2. Time

3. Reason for the Call.

4. Qualifier

5. Book the appointment

6. Post-Close the appointment.

There are six distinct steps to making a successful call and booking a solid appointment that will hold and not cancel. Many of you will want to add or delete or will have a tendency to put your own "spin" on these words. If you are not comfortable with them you should not use them but

I will take you step by step through the psychology of each line and even some of the words. My hope is that you will see how well thought out the script is and that you will use it the way it is written.

The Anatomy Of A Prospecting Call

Now, let's dissect this call line by line so we can see the psychology behind it and why it works.

1. Reminder – You don't make as much of an impression as you thought!

Let's look at the state of mind and the process that your contact goes through when you call them. (I know you want to know your process but we're going to try something new in selling and focus on them!)

Phone Rings: Prospect looks at caller ID. They see your name come up and they don't know right away who you are. Your name might seem a little familiar to them but in most cases they don't remember who you are. They pick up the phone slightly curious and slightly suspicious.

Prospect: "Hello...?"

NM: "Hi John this is Mike Durkin............"

Before you even say the next thing your prospect is doing a file search with a chip in their head faster than anything Bill Gates can design. It looks and sounds like this: "Mike Durkin, Mike Durkin, do I know a Mike Durkin?.......rings a bell but.........?

Sometimes your prospect will instantly recognize your

name but in 90% of the cases they come up with a big yellow triangle that says, "File not found", "File not found." You must be aware that just because you have mentioned your name that your prospect is still extremely suspicious and you don't have much at this point.

NM: "Hi John this is Mike Durkin. I don't know if you remember me but we met last week over at Capriccio's in the lobby when we were waiting for our dinners?"

At this point I am just looking for recognition. I am not looking to be overly warm nor do I want to get to warm and fuzzy right now about whatever we talked about (Remember, how would the Interviewer be acting?) This is a business call and I'm going to treat it as such.

Prospect: (Thinking in their head) "Oh yeah I remember this guy/gal now."

Most people will then form a mental picture of you, the meeting and will come up with a feeling about the encounter. The mistake many Network Marketer's make here is that they expect (hope) that the prospect will respond with a warm, I'm happy that you called me greeting like, "Oh Hi Mike, how are you?" That may be the case but you have to realize there is a lot going on in their heads right now and that may or may not happen. If you don't get a warm response don't panic and quite frankly I don't want you to care. (Remember- would the Interviewer care?) The key here is not to expect that they are going to be excited, friendly or happy that you called. If they are that's okay but don't let it throw you if they aren't.

Prospect: "Oh yeah, I remember you. How are you?"

Many of you are going to hate what I am about to point out next. You will notice the absence of the phrase, "How are you?" It will not destroy your call if you ask them how they are but it won't help you! Some of you will think this is impolite and if you really need to put a "How are you?" into your script. I'm okay with that. However you have to accept that saying, "How are you?" will reduce the effectiveness of your call by about 30%. The use of "How are you?" will also increase the possibility of objections surfacing and the prospect giving you a hard time.

In addition, my use of the phrase, **"I don't know if you remember me but........."** is a very subtle technique called a "paradox question." A paradox question challenges the mind and invokes a response that is stronger than normal. Whenever you tell someone that you don't know if they can do something they will generally show you twice as hard that they can!

2. Time - Stop Trying To Book Appointments With People That Don't Have An Open Mind

When your prospect says, "Oh yeah, I remember you. How are you?" they are thinking two things in parallel:

Prospect (Thinking): "Do I have time for this call right now?"

Your prospect has been making decisions like this all day. If you are calling them at work they are definitely in this mode. Most likely, you are calling them at home so they may be a little more relaxed about it but they will still go through an evaluation process. That process includes sifting through and deciding which things are priorities and which ones need their attention now.

If you have called them at home you have probably interrupted them. Just expect that you have but don't worry about it or be apologetic about it. (Remember- what would the Interviewer say?) They could be cooking dinner, holding a wailing baby, on call waiting with another call on hold or doing all three at the same time. This is what you do in your house don't you? When you call them they are in the process of deciding which thing to do next so you say:

NM: Do you have 30 to 50 seconds to talk?

While this statement seems extremely benign it is effectively Ninja-like and deals with several psychological obstacles that your prospect could have and it eliminates some critical mistakes that Network Marketers make when calling.

1. It is **NOT** apologetic. Many people will say, "Is this a bad time?" or "Did I catch you at a bad time?" Or "I hope I didn't interrupt you?" What would the Interviewer think, say or do if they were calling with a job opportunity? They would be like, "This person better be happy that I took the time to call them at home and they better drop everything to talk with me because this is their one chance and they better not blow it!"

2. Even though you never apologize for calling them at home you must still deal with the fact that you have interrupted them and you want to respect them by asking them: "Do you have 30 to 50 seconds to talk?" This acknowledges that you know they are busy and that you may have called at a bad time but saying it this way leaves you with a strong posture.

3. Asking for "30 to 50 seconds" is somewhat different
and slightly unique. It interrupts the pattern the
most people will use by saying, "Do you have a
minute to talk?" It catches their attention because it
is different but it doesn't throw them off balance
completely. Caution: Don't use any other phrase.
This one works!

4. You are asking permission instead of just rushing in
and rambling on or pitching them. They get calls
from telemarketers constantly where the person on
the other end says hello and then rushes in and
starts their pitch without seeing if the prospect can
or wants to talk. It's disrespectful, rude and people
hate it. You don't want to be grouped together with
telemarketing callers. That's a death knell!

5. If your prospect is burning the chicken, the baby is
biting them on the leg and they are just opening up
a letter from the IRS this may not be the best time
to try to book a meeting with them! By asking them
if they have "30 to 50 seconds" you determine if
they have an open mind. You don't want to be trying to book a meeting with someone that really
didn't want to take the call, can't concentrate at all
and is upset that you are interrupting them. People
answer the phone all the time with no intention of
being able to talk but that's not your fault. You do
have to deal with it, however.

6. By establishing that you need "30 to 50 seconds"
they can now gauge how much time they will need
for your call and determine if they can devote that
time to it. By asking for the "30 to 50 seconds" you
give them the information they need to make a

decision to take the time to listen to you; or not. If they know that you need a short amount of time then they can open their minds and concentrate for THAT amount of time. They will also notice (sub consciously) that you have been very specific about the amount of time you need. Everyone knows that when you ask, "Do you have a minute?" that it will be much longer than that.

7. By establishing YOUR timeline up front you are also letting your prospect know that YOU have limited time. This sends the message that this call is business and not social. That's important because hopefully you did some bonding and rapport stuff with your prospect when you met them. When you skip the bonding and go right to the business you are taking the position of the Interviewer. (Could you imagine an Interviewer asking their applicant how the kids were doing in soccer?) In addition, when you mention that there is a timeline for the call it gives you an excuse to get off the call if they try to corner you with a bunch of questions.

What If They Don't Have The Time?

We've already discussed the subtleties of asking for "30-50 seconds." Let's suppose they say:

Prospect: "I don't have the time to talk, I was just running out the door."

This is not the time to get your 30-50 seconds in. Do you really want to book your appointment with someone who doesn't have 30-50 seconds? You don't. Now it might be "smoke" and they might be using this as an excuse but most prospects quite frankly at this point are more curious than they are suspicious. If they have the time and their head is not totally occupied with the next thing they have to do they will listen. If they tell you that they can't listen I would simply say:

NM: "I understand. When would be a good time to call you back?"

Then get that time and call them back at that time. If they say:

Prospect: "Well I won't be back until tonight. What is this about?"

NM: "Well, since you are running out now's not the time to get into it. I'll find you tonight or call another time, make sense?"

Prospect: "Okay, talk to you later."

If you don't need your prospect to like you can be firm like that and tell THEM how the call is going to go - NOT them telling you how to do it. More on handling objections later.

3. Reason For The Call – They're Thinking It So You Might As Well Get To It!

Now remember that I said there are two things that your prospect is thinking simultaneously? Here's the second one and it is pounding in their head like a native's drum and it won't go away until you answer it and it sounds like this:

Prospect (Thinking): "What does this person want?"

You have to understand that your call is a little unusual because it is proactive. When your prospect casually meets someone they don't really expect to ever hear from that person again. Then a week or so later you call and it's a little weird for them. That's one of the reasons that you want to make sure that your call really has a business tone to it and that you are not too chummy. Another version of what they are thinking is:

Prospect (Thinking): "Why is this person calling?"

So your next line is:

NM: "John the reason for my call is this......."

You have just answered the question that has been nagging in the back of his mind ever since he/she saw your name on his caller ID. In effect you have used a technique that I call "Psychic Salesperson" You have "psychically" read his/her mind and in a small way you have bonded with your prospect by anticipating their question about two seconds before they ask it. It's not the key to selling but it's one of those small Ninja-like moves that is helpful.

It is important to note that I am not including a lot of bonding or chatting here in this script and that it is for a very specific reason. By keeping your conversation rather business-like and efficient you are giving your prospect the impression that this is not the time to be asking questions or getting into a long-winded discussion. If you are doing a lot of bonding they will get the impression that this IS the time to ask you about the opportunity and you will get cornered. I'll show you how to deal with being cornered but why put yourself in that position if you don't have to. If your goal is to book a meeting- just book it!

NM: "John the reason for my call is this: I work with some partners of mine from _____ who have developed a business where we show people how to use the Internet to move goods and services. We've developed a profile of the kind of person that we like to work with and you impressed me as having some of the qualities that we look for. John, when it comes to making money do you keep your options open?

Let's look at the line: **I work with some partners of mine in _____.** (put some out of state name that your upline is in)

Deal Makers Have Their Own Language

In the world of business owners and investors there are certain ways of doing business and there is a vernacular that they use. We've already discussed the words not to use like, "home-based" and "my wife and I." Whenever you discuss your business, even casually, I suggest that you always mention that you have partners. Investors and business owners always have "partners." People that make serious residual income know that they can't do it alone and they are always hooking up with people to get their deals done. Referencing your partners gives you a certain posture and also gives you several tactical advantages when it comes to dealing with objections.

Description Of The Business

Your description of the business should be both clear

and mysterious at the same time. Do not rush through the next sentence or be afraid of any questions. It is important to remember that if you maintain a strong Interviewers posture you are not going to get asked questions anyway.

NM:.....who have developed a business where we show people how to use the internet to move goods and services.

What does this really say? Not much and yet enough! The Internet is a known quantity so there is no question there and many people realize that the Internet is a great untapped opportunity still available. They certainly know that many people are making a ton of money off of the Internet and have probably had the thought that they should too! But of course they don't even know how to get started. You may have to customize this phrase for your business if the Internet example doesn't make sense. It doesn't really matter what it is. Keep it short, simple and somewhat ambiguous. Remember, you don't have to answer ANY of their questions at this point.

NM: ......We've developed a profile of the kind of person that we like to work with and you impressed me as the kind of person that has some of the qualities that we look for.

Remember that you are still in the "reason for the call" stage and that they have another question running through their head and it makes them a little suspicious. That question is: Why me? Telling them that they fit the profile helps them make more sense of the call because if you don't get it that their head is kind of swirling right now you better remember when you got your call from your sponsor. In this sentence is also a subtle "stroke" that you are impressed with them and as long as you don't blow it out of proportion it's a good move and will pump them up a little keeping them interested in the next sentence.

NM:....John, when it comes to making money do you keep your options open?

It is important to ask this question for several reasons but I want you to understand that I am not that concerned about their answer at this point. My main reason for asking this question is that you need to break up the script a bit and stop talking! Get inside your prospect's head for a minute and think about what is happening: In the space of about a minute or so they are processing quite a lot of information at Pentium-like speed. It's busy in their head as they try to digest that this stranger is calling them and talking about some business to them and they are trying to make sense of a lot of who, where, why's and so forth. The answer to the question is not as important as slowing them down. The question also helps to engage them back into the conversation and makes it sound less like you are reading a script.

Prospect: "Yes, No or "What do you have in mind"

4. Qualifier – You're Still Interviewing And This Is No Time To Sound Needy!

NM: Well, What I would need to do is sit down with you for about 40 minutes or so and ask you some questions. Based on your answers I'll know whether or not there's a fit there between us and whether or not I would make a recommendation to my partners and if we should go any further. If I think there's a match there, I'll explain to you how

we work and if it makes sense to you we can go to the next step but if you don't think it fits for you would you be comfortable telling me that it's not a fit for you and that we don't need to go any further – can you tell me "NO?"

This part of the script is ALL about posture and attitude. It takes away the feeling for them that you are trying to sell them something, get them into something or need them! You are being very clear with them about what your meeting/interview will look like and how it will be structured. And of course it is also extremely clear about who is in control!

NM: Well, What I would need to do is sit down with you for about 40 minutes or so and ask you some questions....

You are setting the stage here for the need for a meeting (without calling it a meeting) as well as setting the time parameters. In addition, you are starting the process by stating that you will need to ask them some questions just as an Interviewer does. You maintain control and keep "them" jumping through the hoops: Not YOU jumping through them! This is a huge change from most network–marketing scripts that have you doing anything you can do to "get in front of them" and "show them the opportunity."

NM: Based on your answers I'll know whether or not I would make a recommendation to my partners and if we should go any further. If I think there's match there, I'll explain to you how we work...

The message you are sending to your prospect is that

THEY will need to qualify and that you will be very interested in how they handle themselves and how they answer your questions. This is exactly what the Interviewer does in a job interview and it will give that kind of a "feel" to your prospect. You are also telling them that "IF" they qualify you will explain to them the opportunity that you have. "Showing them how you work" now becomes a "carrot" that they will try to achieve instead of badgering you and getting all suspicious and asking "What is this all about?" Also, mentioning that you will "need to make a recommendation to the partners" puts you in a position of power because you now become the channel for your prospect to impress the "partners." It is essential that you realize that we are doing exactly the opposite of what most Network-Marketing companies suggest and train their distributors to do and that is why it works! We are also setting the stage to make your "showing the business" just that much more powerful and enticing to your prospect but that's for another book.

NM:...and if it makes sense to you we can go to the next step...

With this sentence we now acknowledge that our prospect might actually have some say in what goes on in this interaction also! (How nice of us!) Up until now you have been very tightly controlling the conversation and leading our prospect where we want them to go. Now is the time to relax your stranglehold a little bit on your prospect because I don't want them to feel restricted and controlled. By telling them "if it makes sense to you" you are giving them back some control in the process and it will start to take some pressure off them and put them back (slightly) in the drivers seat.

NM:... if you don't think it fits for you, would you feel comfortable telling me, that it's not a fit for you and that we don't need to go any further - can you tell me "No?"

5. Book The Appointment – What is the "Cloud" that hangs over every potential appointment that keeps you from booking it?

So the question I have for you now is "Why don't prospect's readily invite you in to come and meet with them?" Think about this for a bit before you answer. Here are some of the responses I get in my live seminars:

"They don't want to be sold anything"

"They don't want to feel the pressure to say yes"

"They are afraid they will buy"

"They don't want to buy, make a mistake and feel foolish"

"They don't want to get a sales pitch and feel they have to make a decision"

All good answers and to some degree they are true but the real reason that your prospect doesn't invite you to meet with them is that they are afraid they will have to tell you, "NO"

"Now wait a minute, MJ," you're thinking to yourself. "That can't be why a prospect doesn't invite me in! Saying, 'NO' is the easy part. If they're not interested they can just say so and I'll be on my way, no hard feelings."

Actually saying "NO" is the hardest part and it's why your prospect doesn't invite you in and gives you all kinds of stalls and objections. Let's discuss this in depth.

Let's suppose you get invited into someone's home to show them your opportunity. I'm going to assume for a minute that you are the kind of person that someone would want to have in their home; you are personable, warm, and decent and have integrity. You are in fact a pleasant and respectful person. Now, let's continue to imagine that you start to have this "interaction" with your prospect. Perhaps you find something you have in common like children or hobbies. You take a sincere interest in them and ask them some questions about them and they feel comfortable talking with you. In fact they begin to warm up to you and they like you. In fact they are really enjoying being around you and your positive energy. Now, what is the best way for them to "consummate" this "love affair"? Of course it's to say, "YES" to you. It's to "buy" whatever you are selling because it affirms your relationship. Saying "YES" is the easy part! Buying from you is the fun part because it says, "I like you, agree with you and we get to continue our relationship!"

The hard part is saying "NO" Let's suppose all the previous things we imagined are true; they like you, you've bonded with them etc. They now have a BIG problem! If they have to say no to you it is going to get very uncomfortable for them because even your prospects have a need for approval and need you to like them! And since they just became your best buddy it is really tough for them to tell you that they would rather clean septic systems then get involved in some network-marketing scheme and ask their friends to buy personal care items.

Your prospects have been in this situation before. They have invited salespeople into their home and office and they have felt this pressure when they need to say, "NO" to people that they like. So they have developed a self-defense move that keeps them out of this uncomfortable situation. **That move is to not invite you to come to see them in the first place!** That way there won't be pressure and they will not have to feel uncomfortable telling you anything negative.

So it's not that your prospects are afraid of saying, "Yes" and "buying" what you have but it's that they are afraid to say, "No" to you. They can't handle the idea that you will think poorly of them.

NM: ...but if you don't think it fits for you would you be comfortable telling me, that it's not a fit for you and that we don't need to go any further - can you tell me "No?"

You have just eliminated your prospect's largest fear to meeting with you and looking at your Network Marketing opportunity or a proposal for world peace for that matter! There is no reason for them not to meet with you and look at something because you have told them that not only are you willing to hear "NO" but you actually want THEM to be okay with telling you "NO."

It will be a little tough saying the last line the first couple of times. All of your training (if you've had the misfortune of being classically trained) will rebel against the idea of allowing, even encouraging the prospect to say "NO" Your own inner voice will scream, "But I want them to like me and see the benefits and be excited and say, "YES", I don't even want to bring up the idea of saying "NO."

When you give your prospect the freedom to say "NO" to you a magical thing happens. First of all they are confused and that's a good thing because they have never heard an approach like this before. You don't sound like every other network-marketing pit bull they've encountered before. So you've interrupted the pattern but you've also removed every single objection and reason that they could logically think up to keep you away. You have rendered their self-defense system powerless and they really are somewhat flummoxed because they really don't know what to say. Here are some of the responses that I have heard when I have said to a prospect, "Are you comfortable with telling me "NO?"

"Did you just ask me to tell you "NO"?

"No problem. Telling people "NO" is one of my best things!"

"Well if you're okay with me telling you "NO" come on in, it's your funeral."

"Okay with telling you "NO?" I'll tell you to get the heck out of my office!"

"You WANT me to say "NO" to you? I can do that"

"Sure I can tell you "NO" When do you want to get together?"

It is essential for you to realize that you must deliver the line from the script exactly as it is written. It must be delivered in the form of a direct question where you force them to answer. If you mess with the line by putting it forth as a statement such as "If there isn't a fit there you can just say "NO" you will reduce your effectiveness in booking a meeting by over 50%. Trust MJ on this one! Let's look at the next line in the script:

Prospect: "Sure, I can tell you No."

NM: "Good. Do you have your calendar handy?"
Prospect: "I'll get it...........Okay it's in front of me."

NM: "Good. Now I could come to your place if that's easy for you or we could meet somewhere for coffee. Which is better for you?"

With deference to J. Douglas Edwards, Dale Carnegie, Zig Ziglar and Tom Hopkins I just had to throw a memorial "alternate of choice" close in there somewhere!

Prospect: "I guess meeting for coffee would be fine"

NM: "That's good. Now my schedule only gives me a chance to meet with you after work hours. Would right after work, say around 5:30PM or so work?

Prospect: "That's fine."

NM: "How about the diner on West Street?"

Prospect: "Yes, I know that place."

NM: "Good. Now, my schedule's pretty tight this

week. Does Tuesday work or is Thursday better for you?"

Again, I am not being easy about my schedule, how it's wide open and I'm just dying to book one meeting so I can tell my upline that I did it! Successful people are busy and their schedules are tight. Don't say, "Well any night is okay for me. Which one do you want?" Make them work for it.

Prospect: "Tuesday is good for me."
NM: "Okay, so I'm writing you down in my book for Tuesday at 5:30PM at the diner on West Street. John, before I go is there any reason you wouldn't consider this to be a confirmed, solid appointment?"

There are a number of nuances to discuss about this seemingly benign paragraph but first let's deal with the logistics. In my seminars I always get the questions, "When do you call to confirm?" "How do I eliminate driving an hour, sitting in a diner for a hour, getting 'no-showed', getting depressed and going home with another night wasted?" I always give them my number and tell them to call me if something comes up. Is that the right thing to do?" "Should you confirm the day before or the night before?"

Giving a prospect your number in case something comes up almost guarantees something will come up. Calling the day before to confirm is weak – and it means that you set up a weak appointment and it increases the possibility by 50% that your prospect is going to postpone. It also raises the possibility that they will start to ask questions and come up with objections.

RULE: IF YOU SET UP A STRONG APPOINTMENT WITH CONFIDENCE AND POST-CLOSE THE APPOINT-MENT YOU SHOULD NEVER OFFER YOUR NUMBER OR CALL TO CONFIRM. PERIOD!

What do most Network Marketers do the minute the prospect says, "YES" and they agree to a meeting? They try as quickly as they can to jump off the phone so the prospect doesn't change their mind! Don't deny it. You know it's true and it's a huge mistake. This is a great opportunity to solidify your posture. Would the Interviewer jump off the call afraid of another question or objection? No. Would they cross their fingers and just hope that the applicant showed up? No. When you say to your prospect:

NM:.... John, before I go is there any reason you wouldn't consider this to be a confirmed, solid appointment?

You are sending a strong and clear message. That message is that you are confident enough in who you are to give them an opportunity to back out right now if they need to! It's important that you understand the powerful psychology behind what you have just done. You have just clearly established control by relinquishing control. Remember that "Dealmakers" never beg people to meet with them to get involved with their projects. (Can you imagine Donald Trump saying to a potential investor, "Let me give you my number so you can call me in case some-thing comes up"?) They give their prospects the impres-sion that if they want in on the great potential of the deal that they better be impressive – and that means showing up and on time!

When you ask this powerful paradox question of a prospect it signals to them that you expect them to be there and if they answer in the affirmative then they have just committed to the appointment – again!
So, our prospect answers:

Prospect: "No it's definite"

NM: "Good. I'll meet you in the lobby of the diner at 5:30 on Tues. See you then.
I then give them a visual by repeating the time and then a description of where I will meet them. If I was going to someone's home I would say:

NM: Good. I'll be on the doorstep of your house at 5:30 on Tues. See you then.

Here is the script in its entirety:

Prospect: "Hello?"

**NM: "Hi John this is _____.
I don't know if you remember me but we met over at Capriccio's in the lobby when we were waiting for our dinners?"**

Prospect: "Oh yeah, I remember you. How are you?"

NM: "Good. John, Do you have 30 to 50 seconds to talk?"

Prospect: "Sure. Go ahead."

NM: "John the reason for my call is this: I work

with some partners of mine from _____
who have developed a business where we show
people how to use the Internet to move goods and
services. We've developed a profile of the kind of
person that we like to work with and you impressed
me as having some of the qualities that we look for.
John, when it comes to making money do you keep
your options open?"

Prospect: "Yes, No or "What do you have in mind?"
NM: Well, What I would need to do is sit down with
you for about 40 minutes or so and ask you some
questions. Based on your answers, I'll know
whether or not there's a fit there between us and
whether or not I would make a recommendation to
my partners and see if we should go any further. If
I think there's a match there, I'll explain to you how
we work and if it makes sense to you we can go to
the next step, but if you don't think it fits for you
would you be comfortable telling me that it's not a
fit for you and that we don't need to go any further
- can you tell me "No?"

Prospect: "Sure, I can tell you No!"

NM: "Good. Do you have your calendar handy?"

Prospect: "I'll go get it.............Okay it's in front of
me."

NM: "Okay good. Now I could come to your place
if that's easy for you or we could meet somewhere
for coffee. Which is better for you?"

Prospect: "I guess meeting for coffee would be fine."

NM: "That's good for me. Now my schedule only gives me a chance to meet with you after work hours. Would right after work, say around 5:30PM or so work?"

Prospect: "That's fine."

NM: "How about the diner on West Street?"
Prospect: "Yes, I know that the place."

NM: "Good. Now, my schedule's pretty tight this week. Does Tuesday work or is Thursday better for you?

Prospect: "Tuesday is good for me"

NM: "Okay, so I'm writing you down in my book for Tuesday at 5:30PM at the diner on West Street. John, before I go, is there any reason you wouldn't consider this to be a confirmed, solid appointment?"

Prospect: "No, it's definite"

NM: "Good. I'll meet you in the lobby of the diner at 5:30PM on Tues. See you then."

ACTIVITY TRACKER

NM Name _____

Week of _____ thru _____

Daily Activity Goal _____

Consistency Rating (0-10)   0=No dials
                             10=Dials meet Activity Goal

	Activity Goal	#Dials	Consistency Rating
Mon _____ th			
Tues _____ th			
Wed _____ th			
Thurs _____ th			
Fri _____ th			
Sat _____ th			
Sun _____ th			

Week of _____

Consistency Rating for the Week (0-10) _____

NOTES:

ACTIVITY TRACKER - (sample)

NM Name John Sanders

Week of July 11th 2005

Daily Activity Goal 5

Consistency Rating (0-10)   0=No dials

10=Dials meet Activity Goal

	Activity Goal	#Dials	Consistency Rating
Mon 11th	5	////	10
Tues 12th	5	////	10
Wed 13th	5	///	6
Thurs 14th	5	0	0
Fri 15th	5	////	10
Sat 16th	5	/	2
Sun 17th	5	/////////	10

Week of

July 11th

Consistency Rating for the

Week (0-10)

5

NOTES:

Out of a 70-point scale our NM hit 48. He gives himself a "5" for a consistency rating.

NOTES

NOTES

_____

_____

_____

_____

_____

_____

_____

_____

_____

_____

_____

_____

_____

_____

_____

_____

NOTES